WHEN NINJAS

WHEN NINJAS ATTACK

A SURVIVAL GUIDE FOR DEFENDING YOURSELF AGAINST THE SILENT ASSASSINS

SAM KAPLAN
PHOEBE BRONSTEIN
KEITH RIEGERT

ILLUSTRATIONS BY MIRO SALAZAR

Ulysses Press

Published by:
Ulysses Press
P.O. Box 3440
Berkeley, CA 94703
www.ulyssespress.com

ISBN: 978-1-56975-718-5
Library of Congress Control Number: 2009902015

Printed in Canada by Transcontinental Printing
10 9 8 7 6 5 4 3 2 1

Acquisitions Editor: Nick Denton-Brown
Managing Editor: Claire Chun
Editor: Richard Harris
Copyeditor: Lily Chou
Design and layout: what!design @ whatweb.com
Interior ilustrations: Miro Salazar except on page 6 © Keith Riegert
Cover illustration: © istockphoto.com/Gerville

Distributed by Publishers Group West

CONTENTS

INTRODUCTION
The Modern Ninja Threat. 7

CHAPTER 1
A Brief Yet Incredibly Detailed History of the Ninja 13

CHAPTER 2
Know the Ninja. 29

CHAPTER 3
Detecting a Ninja 43

CHAPTER 4
Defending against a Ninja Attack 57

CHAPTER 5
Bugging Out—Making Your Escape 83

CHAPTER 6
Going on the Offense:
Modern Tactics and the Ninja 95

CHAPTER 7
Buying Time: Negotiating with and
Befriending Your Ninja Assassin 105

CHAPTER 8
Ninja Myth and Reality. 113

CHAPTER 9
Conclusion 123

ABOUT THE AUTHORS 127

A ninja prepares to strike an unsuspecting dinner patron.
Hamamatsu, Japan, c. 1870. From the authors' collection.

INTRODUCTION

THE MODERN
NINJA THREAT

If you come to a fork in a road, grab a knife.
—*Proverb found at the Oyaji Ninjutsu School
Hachimantai, Japan, c. 15th century A.D.*

✳ ✳ ✳

Ninja. The word itself evokes feelings of childish awe and absolute terror. The dictionary defines *ninja* as "one trained in the art of *ninjutsu.*" Then, *ninjutsu* is cryptically defined as "the art of stealth." Translated more clearly in English, the term means "what you will not see until it is too late."

Some people believe ninjas are only a Hollywood myth, but the reality is far darker and more dangerous. Ninjas not only plague modern society—they're *everywhere.* They travel undetected across our borders. They hide in our homes and offices. They're spies, tricksters and mercenaries, killing at the behest of maddened laymen, then slipping unheard and unseen from scenes of heinous mayhem.

This book tells you how to live free of the ninja threat. Even as you read these words, your life may already be in grave danger. Take a look around you. Do you see any ninjas? Of course not. The true skill of the ninja is his or her ability to hide in plain sight.

Range of documented ninja activities, 1600–1700 A.D.

Range of documented ninja activities, 1800–2000 A.D.

Maybe you're reading this guide in a coffee shop. See that surly black-clad goth at the counter ordering a peppermint tea? Hardly a disguise. The geeky college student with the glasses, seemingly lost in her MacBook . . . . See that elegantly carved cane leaning against her chair?

Or perhaps you're reading this book out loud to your friends in the comfort of your own living room. You're probably safe, right? Not so fast. Your best friend may be a ninja assassin who for years has patiently awaited the perfect opportunity to poison you or slice your stomach open.

Or worse yet, perhaps you're alone, reading in the privacy of your bedroom. Your windows are shut. Your doors are locked. Surely you're safe. Surely. . . .

Throughout history, ninja activity has never been completely documented. Those who have tried have been killed, "committed suicide" or simply vanished from the face of the earth. Our oversimplified "Hollywood" image of these highly trained human shadows (garbed in black from head to toe, faces covered, carrying martial arts weapons) distract the general public from the reality of the ninja peril. This blissful ignorance is compounded by historians who claim that ninjas disappeared centuries ago. While "terrorist threat levels" remain perpetually orange (high), most people remain joyfully unaware of the constant danger of sudden, catastrophic ninja attacks.

MURDER BY NUMBERS

In the United States, 87 percent of all unsolved murders in the lower 48 states are the direct result of ninja attacks. In Hawaii and Alaska, geographically closer to the ninja home islands of Japan, that figure jumps to 93 percent and 92 percent, respectively.

The power of the ninja is rooted in its difference from modern terrorist and government war machines. Ninjas have no use for the mass media. They perpetually fly under the radar, never seeking notoriety or slipping haphazardly into the public eye. They're serial killers with no modus operandi, who make no mistakes. Ninjas have no allegiance, not even the

Bushido code, and they have no regard for your life or their own. A ninja's own death comes, usually by his or her own hand, with the dishonor of failing in a mission. For the ninja, failure means just one thing—the intended victim is still breathing, still twitching, still alive.

WHY ME?

The first thing you'll ask yourself before or during a ninja attack is, "Why would a ninja attack *me*?" The fact is everyone is a potential ninja target. Ninjas are hired assassins and can be employed for reasonable prices. Therefore, anyone may hire a ninja against you—be it a neglected lover, envious coworker, disgruntled employee or someone who simply "doesn't like the cut of your jib." If you lead a pious, sin-free life, you have a good chance of avoiding a ninja attack. Of course, as the old adage says, nobody's perfect.

ANATOMY OF A NINJA ATTACK

9 MONTHS AND 1 DAY UNTIL ATTACK: You "accidentally" consume the last bagel at work in front of the intern who drove half an hour to pick them up. Thus, you deny her breakfast. The intern hires a ninja to settle the score.

9 MONTHS: After negotiating a few clauses and signing and counter-signing contracts, a ninja team is dispatched to your hometown. They establish an outpost at your neighborhood Baja Fresh.

8 MONTHS, 21 DAYS: The ninja team begins daily reconnaissance operations, stealthily posting one ninja in your house, one at your workplace and one along your commute.

8 MONTHS, 15 DAYS: The ninja team has now established a thorough timetable of your routine. They can anticipate your whereabouts with 87 percent accuracy.

7 MONTHS: The ninja squad is now intimately familiar with your entire schedule; they're beginning to understand your inner psyche.

continued on next page

continued from previous page

4 MONTHS: Nothing about you is secret. Over carnitas burritos, the ninjas often laugh about your unpleasant tendency to vigorously scratch your groin while you sleep.

3 MONTHS, 16 DAYS: The ninjas, confident in their covert operations, take an extended vacation, easing any paranoid suspicions you may have as they get some much-needed ninja R & R. (Take this opportunity to finish reading this book and ninja-proof your home, workplace and body. Consider changing genders.)

8 DAYS, 14 HOURS: The ninja team takes up position, reconfirming your daily routine over the next week.

NINJA-NIGHT, 24 MINUTES: You enter your home after a long day of work. The lights are off. You pour a glass of wine, open a jar of red-pepper hummus and turn on the TV.

N-NIGHT, 2 MINUTES: One member of the ninja team initiates the attack, leaving his perch above your bedroom door. The other team members stand guard.

N-NIGHT, ZERO HOUR: The attack ninja unsheathes his sword soundlessly. He draws the sharpened blade to your neck. The TV flickers to a commercial. The soft couch pulls you into a state of deep relaxation. The sword rises, catching the light of the tube. The TV screen faintly reflects the illuminated blade. Are you ready?

CHAPTER 1

A BRIEF YET INCREDIBLY DETAILED HISTORY OF THE NINJA

It has been said that the ninja was born of the samurai's sword.
Not so, the ninja was spawned only of the four true elements: blood,
sweat, tears and more blood.

—*Professor Stephen Eaton-Jones, Ph.D., North Tokyo University Extension*

✳ ✳ ✳

In the beginning, there were *samurai*. These early ass-kicking
warriors were Japan's original military elite, and they dominated the
island nation's battlefields for centuries.

Then, like the razor-sharp egg that exploded mercilessly from the
chicken, came the ninja.

Ninja and samurai share many common characteristics—
proficiency in a variety of martial arts and weaponry, incomparable
libidos and the mental capacity to murder on command. But their
purposes and tactics could not be more different.

RISE OF THE SAMURAI

Toward the end of the 8th century, Japan entered a period of violent political turmoil that would last for centuries. Despotic lords constantly vied for political and geographical control of various regions. Raids, ferocious battles and mayhem came at these fledgling rulers from every direction. The scent of danger was as savagely milky as unfiltered *sake*. A class of loyal military nobility—the *samurai*—rose to meet the military threats. They were highly skilled warriors devoted to a single overlord. The samurai honed their military, political and cultural expertise over the centuries, steadily raising their status throughout Japan.

THE SAMURAI AT WAR

The military prowess of the samurai inspired as much awe as any fighting force in history. When the Mongols attempted to invade Japan with an army of more than 40,000 in 1274, a samurai force of only 10,000 soundly defeated them. Seven years later, the Mongols returned with four times the men. Again, the smaller samurai force demonstrated exactly what *kusokurae shine* truly means.

As the skill, effectiveness and status of samurai forces increased, feudal lords with smaller armies searched for new ways to defeat their enemies. A group of savage Buddhist mountain farmers from the Iga Togo province rose to meet the demand. Training in secret, they became the samurai's equal in combat.

However, unlike the samurai, they held no allegiances but to themselves and could offer their mercenary services to the highest bidder. Without a need for honor, the new warriors became proficient in the arts forbidden to the samurai—concealment, sabotage, espionage and reconnaissance.

These new warriors became infamous for their incredible endurance, sexual stamina, and perseverance of both body and mind.

In time, they would become known as "the blade of the heart," "the whisperer of frightening phrases," *"shinobi-no-mono,"* "persons of stealth," the *nin-ja.*

For the next 700 years, long after the demise of the samurai culture that spawned their existence, the ninja would dominate the professions of espionage and assassination. Their tactics changed little over generations, but their strength and skill blossomed into a raw, powerful force.

Shortly after the advent of ninja techniques, schools dedicated to the martial art of *ninjutsu* began to appear in the Japanese countryside and fledgling cities. Franchises of the best schools sprang up around the world like clandestine fast-food chains.

NINJUTSU: THE ART OF THE NINJA

The ninja training regimen of the early 16th century reads like a manual for training today's elite military Special Forces—that is, if the military's Special Forces were trained from birth. The young ninjas, who inherited their role as silent assassins, had to master no less than 20 warrior skills, some of which were never known to their samurai counterpoints.

First was a conditioned awareness that was developed in infancy. Ninja toddlers were taught to be meticulously aware of everything around them.

As they developed into preteens, they went through the grueling process of rebuilding the inner being. The aspiring ninjas' spirits were broken, their personalities erased. In time they would see only through the perspective of ninja. Fledgling ninjas were rigorously taught to evaluate their mission in calculations, not feelings, processing information the way their ninja master would.

Throughout history, Japan's occasionally severe weather delivered lethal blows to adversaries who attempted to invade the islands. The winds were known by many as the mystical *kame-no-kaze* and later *kamekaze*, or "wind of the gods." But in the Iga and Kiga regions of Japan, it was widely known that the winds blew at the behest of the ninja—and the ninja alone.

NINE LEVELS OF PERSONAL GROWTH

For the ninja, there are nine levels of personal growth that can be broken down into three broad phases.

PHASE I (STEPS 1-3): DISCIPLINING THE BODY

Phase I is primarily concerned with physical development. Training begins during gestation; late in the second trimester, parents begin to encourage strong fetal kicks and other sharp movements by petting the stomach and feeding the fetus special treats on days the kicks are strongest. Ninjas continue to discipline their bodies for their entire lifetime, but primary developmental training exercises are generally completed by late adolescence. Balance, strength, endurance, and unarmed and armed combat are all thoroughly honed. The final aspect of Phase I is silence—running, jumping, eating and fighting without making a sound. Once trainees master Phase I, they officially earn the title of *ninja*.

PHASE II (STEPS 4-6): DISCIPLINING THE MIND

The beginning stages of Phase II can be closely aligned with the Western concept of "self-control." In order to pass this phase, ninjas must first learn to take full control of their own mind, learning various methods that will help recognize and subdue dangerous emotions such as anger, jealousy, greed, fear and lust. Finally, once they've learned to control their own mind, they can begin to manipulate the minds of their enemies.

The rising Phase II ninjas must also train to heighten their sensitivity and awareness. They must learn to ascertain important environmental information by maximizing all five of senses.

Learning to use the proximity senses is vital, as it enables the ninja to spy, track and fight an opponent in utter darkness.

A ninja who has mastered this phase should be capable of blinded navigation and warfare with equal skill and precision as a novice ninja in broad daylight.

PHASE III (STEPS 7-9): UNDERSTANDING THE UNIVERSE

The final phase of ninja training is the hardest to reach and also the most difficult to grasp. To become a Phase III student, the ninja must learn to understand, predict and manipulate the "vibrant force of the universe." This universal force is not one that most Westerners can begin to fathom. It's neither tangible nor scientifically observable, but once harnessed, provides the individual with profound power. The ninja who has mastered Phase III possesses an arsenal of mysterious skills, including the ability to inflict pain without touch and instinctively demoralize an opponent through private insecurities.

The "Death Force" is another aspect of the universe understood exclusively by Phase III ninjas. When someone formulates a plan to kill another person, he or she releases a "Death Force," similar to pheromones or "bad vibes." The advanced Phase III ninja can detect an opponent's imminent strike by sensing increased levels of this force.

Experts agree that Phases II and III separate ninjas from other martial-arts experts. Although many forms of combat training emphasize mental and spiritual growth, *ninjutsu* places them above all else, delivering the ninja's immense power and eternal mystery.

Next, trainees were taught the ferocious art of ninja hand-to-hand combat. They learned to punch, kick, grapple, strangle and escape without making a sound or elevating their breathing or heartbeat.

The young ninjas then learned the sciences of brewing tea, meteorology, navigation and terrain. By understanding their world with profound intimacy, ninjas gained confidence in their movements until it was impossible for them to get lost at land or sea. As they came to understand the smallest changes in weather patterns, they could even take advantage of the air itself.

Schooling in an extensive arsenal of weaponry followed the first flush of puberty. The ninjas becoming proficient in handling swords, daggers and knives, throwing stars, spears, staffs, chains, nunchucks and explosives. Their bodies grew immensely to meet the physical demands of their heavy, copious weaponry. This gave them the physical brawn and long, ropey muscles characteristic of their sexy image to this day.

Finally, the ninjas refined their skills in stealthy movement and transportation. They learned the arts of espionage, concealment, disguise, climbing and covert escape. They learned to travel by land and water with speed unmatched by any medieval knight. In order to build patience and become comfortable in what most would consider uncomfortable positions, the ninjas would spend hours sitting in small boxes placed around their village.

As a final test before earning the title of *ninja,* students were required to enter a rival lord's house at night, steal into the man's bed chambers and remove a solitary molar from the sleeping man's mouth. Many paintings depicting notorious ninjas show the stolen molars strung around their necks, the first of many secret decorations the ninjas would earn.

NINJA WEAPONRY

The artistic, immaculately crafted weapons of the ninja deliver as much awe as they do death. Fashioned out of carefully folded, ultra-strong steel, finely woven fibers and the rarest of Eastern plant life, these implements of destruction are among the world's most exquisite.

Ninja-to (Sword)

When most people think of the ninja sword, they imagine the artful, cherished blades used by the samurai. While the *ninja-to*, with its gently curved shape and unbreakable steel construction, bears strong similarities, it's not as long nor as revered as the samurai sword. From its plain black hilt and grip to the unmarked steel shaft and ordinary scabbard, the ninja sword has always been considered a tool for lethal combat, nothing more. Razor sharp and capable of devastating slash

and jab strikes, the *ninja-to* is guaranteed to kill you. The carefully crafted blade is so strong that it can cut through steel, concrete and hope. Your best bet to defend against a razor-sharp *ninja-to* would be a full-body shield made of diamond-strengthened steel.

Shuriken (Throwing Blades)

Known to Westerners as "ninja stars," *shuriken* are the most overtly intimidating weapons employed by the ninja. Although the blades, rarely over two inches long, generally do not deliver lethal stab wounds, a quick strike from a medium distance is demoralizing at best and often physically paralyzing. If confronted by a ninja, expect a hail of *shuriken* throughout the battle, not just the beginning. Even when holding a drawn sword in the throwing hand, a ninja can throw a star with the other hand, thanks to years of ambidexterity training. Effective present-day defenses against *shuriken* almost always involve Kevlar, a lightweight, durable synthetic that dramatically reduces the damage of thrown blades, although they can be ineffective at close range.

Bo, *Jo* and *Hambo* (Wooden Staffs)

Most people can "carry a big stick," but few know how to wield it properly. Ninjas do. The ninja staff comes in a variety of lengths—the three-foot *hambo*, the four-foot *jo* and the six-foot *bo*—and all are highly effective fighting weapons. The strike to be most wary of is the full-force blow from the end of a staff. Ninjas rely heavily on such thrust blows to incapacitate their victims, concentrating enormous power into a small, deadly tip. Wallops to the head, back or vital organs, along with the thrusts, make the staff a versatile whacking weapon. Ninjas are also trained to use household objects as fighting staffs. Always keep your broom and mop handles in a locked, secure area. It may make sweeping and cleaning a little less convenient, but it could spell the difference between life and death—or at least a few broken ribs.

Yumi (Ninja Bow and Arrow)

When it comes to sniping, the highly covert ninja bow (*yumi*) is only slightly less effective than the M40A3 sniper rifle employed by the U.S. Marines. Both the twang of the bowstring and distinctive midflight arrow whistle have been dampened with reeds to sink below the range of human hearing, making the ninja sniper a completely silent assassin. The compact bow can be slacked and slipped into a thin piece of hollow bamboo or blueprint tube, unnoticeable in a crowd of architects. According to eyewitness accounts, from a "tiger-crouch" firing position, ninja bowmen have hit targets up to 1,000 meters away.

Because of the relatively slow speed of an arrow compared to a bullet, if you spot a sniper you may have enough time to cover your face, heart and neck, robbing the assassin of a sure-kill shot.

Ninja arrows can pierce double-paned, vacuum-sealed glass, as well as car windows. When you're at home, keep your shades drawn at all times, especially on the second floor, where a ninja is most likely to strike. Fashion "car curtains" that you can draw closed whenever you're stopped at a light or caught in dense traffic.

Concealed Blades and Weapons

Notorious tricksters, ninjas almost always carry concealed weapons. One of the most common is the *shinobi-zue*. A once-commonplace gentlemen's accessory in Western society, this common cane/walking stick can be hollowed out and the handle fitted with a blade up to three feet long. The straight blade can be wielded just as effectively as a sword. So be extremely wary of any "old man" sporting a walking stick or cane.

Another form of weaponry oft concealed in *shinobi-zue* are weighted chains used for swinging strikes or ensnaring limbs. A cane can also be used to shoot poison darts, removing both end caps to reveal a blowgun. A single, well-placed dart that hits an artery can mean permanent lights-out.

Never turn your back on a person with a cane, no matter what the distance. If you encounter someone carrying one, pay special attention to the cane's make and shape. Cylindrical metal canes are light and durable, perfect for dart guns. Larger wooden canes may contain hidden blades. Canes with a platform base and some "walkers" can conceal weighted chains or narrow *shuriken*.

EXPLOSIVES, SMOKE BOMBS AND POWDERS

Originally designed to dazzle, confuse and demoralize their opponents, ninja explosives and powders have evolved into a deadly art all their own. Powders to blind or intoxicate victims are often inserted into the delicate eggs of the *tancho*, or Japanese crane, which the ninja hurls at unsuspecting opponents, incapacitating them. Blinding solutions can be as simple as dirt and fine thorns mixed with crushed *sansho* pepper. More advanced, mind-altering powders often combine blinding solution with finely ground hallucinogenic mushrooms. Fighting back after being affected by either is nearly impossible. And death is just a bit more terrifying.

Smoke bombs conceal a ninja's position and can also be packed with high-grade *asa* (cannabis). Refrain from inhaling when passing through *any* cloud of smoke. Ninjas who have meticulously rid their bodies of THC receptors, will not be affected, though they may *appear* more relaxed.

UNARMED COMBAT

It's often said that an animal is most dangerous when it's trapped. Without room to run, strike or fight, the beast's fear-heightened adrenaline level makes it ferocious. While "fear" is unknown to the ninja, a ninja caught without weapons is just as dangerous as one armed to the teeth.

Hand-to-hand ninja training is the most rigorous in the world. Like Indochina's top Muay Thai fighters, ninjas spend years physically hardening their bodies through repeated abuse—head-butting suspended boulders, sharpening their claw attacks on granite faces, splitting dense hardwood trunks with thunderous punches.

Phalanges Strikes

The most debilitating strikes are those delivered with the fingers, thumbs, knuckles or toes, which concentrate the full force of the rocketing limb into the smallest possible area. A toe strike to the ribs can puncture a lung. A *shikan-ken* (extended-finger-knuckle strike) to the neck can shatter the trachea. The aquiline-nosed ninja may even use his beaked face to strike at the opponent's eyes or groin.

Consider every body part of the ninja capable of dealing a death blow. Remember to sidestep a punch, kick or head butt to reduce its efficacy and force. Do not attempt to grapple on the ground with a ninja. If you have testicles, a ninja *will* kick you there. Guard your head and vital organs and fight back vigorously.

NINJA GEAR

Like the ninja's lethal weaponry, the gear they use is carefully crafted, lightweight and extremely efficient in getting the job done. You'll be surprised by where a ninja can manage to hide.

Jika-Tabi

Ninjas today still wear *jika-tabi*, the same style of footwear they donned in the era of the shogun. These split-toe boots resemble the type used for diving and surfing with Western wetsuits. While affording little protection from sharp objects, the shoes aid the ninja's ability to climb ropes, trees and walls. Their lightweight and soft bottoms also ensure stealthy entry.

Climbing Wear

To move from walls to ceilings, as well as up trees or telephone poles, ninjas will also strap on *aishiki*, small spikes that affix to the soles of their shoes, much like Western crampons used in rock climbing. These metal spikes hinder ground movement and are about as difficult to remove as Western ski boots, so if you're faced with a ninja wearing *aishiki*, take advantage of the few precious seconds before they remove them and make a break. *Do not* attempt to fight a ninja wearing *aishiki*. A spiked kick can be devastating, especially to an exposed face or lightly clad sex organs.

Similar to the *aishiki* on the feet, *shuku*, or "tiger claws," are worn on the hands to aid in climbing. Strapped around the wrist and palm with a thick piece of leather connecting the straps, the handgrips have two fang-like spikes that curve down from the fingers toward the forearm. While the grips make for superb climbing and a potentially painful open-hand slap, they inhibit the ninja's ability to wield a sword. Again, take advantage of the moments it takes a ninja to remove his or her climbing gear. Make a quick escape.

NINJA HIERARCHY

The complex cultural structure of a ninja society has its roots in the very beginning of *ninjutsu*. The strict hierarchical organization is almost identical today as it was at the turn of the 18th century.

Jonin: Each *ryu* (ninja school or clan) is structured much like a modern corporation or military. At the top of the ninja pyramid is the *jonin*—the ultimate ninja. The *jonin*, usually a white-bearded elder, has passed all nine levels of personal development, and is a veritable Phase III ninja. The *jonin* knows the ways of the world. Through an immense global network of field agents, he has intimate insider information about important people in every corner of the world. It takes no fewer than 85 years for a ninja to become a *jonin*.

Chunin: Below the *jonin* are the *chunin*. *Chunin* are akin to the rank of colonels—with each *ryu* promoting a few ninjas to the rank. *Chunin* are usually advanced Phase II or beginning Phase III ninjas who have proven their loyalty to their clan through the most trying of circumstances, and have shown superior combat skills.

Genin: *Chunin* hand out the *jonin*'s orders to field agents known as *genin*; these underlings are the ones who execute specific assignments—espionage, theft, sabotage, reconnaissance and assassination. In order to protect the identity of members of the *ryu*, most *genin* never know the identity of their *jonin*. Oftentimes, multiple *genin* will be given assignments related to the same mission (one will be sent out for reconnaissance, another for sabotage) without knowing each other's involvement. The *jonin* is usually the only ninja who knows the absolute goal of the greater mission.

Temp Workers: In addition to the established members of the ninja clan, *ryu* will often hire third parties for specific, temporary assignments. These temp agents may not be trained ninjas at all. The *ryu* may, for example, hire the house cleaner of their target to perform an easy task. It's possible to find ninja-run temp agencies in foreign countries where *ninjutsu* is not outright outlawed.

JUNO HAGAMUTSI AND HIS INFAMOUS STOMACH CRUSH

According to legend, Juno Hagamutsi, the most notorious ninja of the 17th century, was 4'11" and so heavy that he had an extra layer of fat on each pinky toe. He was rumored to have 42 arm rolls, each deadlier than the last. While this *debu ninja* (literally "fat ass-assin") was not as fast or agile as most of his contemporaries, he equaled history's greatest ninjas in stealth, flexibility and strength, and surpassed almost all in his close-range combat skills. He was rumored to easily absorb fists, feet, daggers and *shuriken* with his immense flesh without injury. Juno's finishing move is considered among the most effective ever conceived; once his opponent was immobilized, Juno would catapult himself into the air and plummet onto his opponent, with his bulbous toes pointed at the abdomen. It is believed over 1,200 victims fell to the infamous "stomach crush."

THE NINJA TODAY

The art of the ninja has changed little from the form that existed in the middle of the last millennium. Out of strict cultural adherence, the ninja does not use modern firearms, technology or body armor. These are an ancient people, steeped in mystery, shrouded in darkness.

To be *ninja* is an inherited trait, much like ethnic makeup, genetic mutation or eye color—it's not a profession or hobby that can be pursued. Without any biological ninja ancestry, it's difficult to become a ninja. Today's Western *dojos* may train you in the "art of *ninjutsu*," but this modernized version is a far cry from the true form.

Perhaps the most dangerous myth about the ninja is that they no longer exist. Most literature and film pertaining to ninjas, *ninjutsu*, and ninja history are either set in a by-gone era, or are unrealistic and comical, leading Americans to believe that ninjas are a relic of Japan's feudal history or, worse, dominated by campy sewer-dwelling turtles. Ninjas have done nothing to dispel their purported extinction as it only serves to make their work that much easier.

THE TAMATAMA RYU AND AMERICA'S WAR ON NINJAS

Much like the failed "War on Drugs" and ongoing "War on Terrorism," the United States has waged a troubled "War on Ninjas" on and off for the last 50-odd years. In 1987, the U.S. government launched a top-secret program called Project STEALTH. Until now, the project has been operated without any public knowledge and with similar information-collecting interests as the CIA, the FBI and the Department of Homeland Security. Project STEALTH, unlike its broad-reaching counterpoints, is exclusively interested in tracking and containing the ninja threat within U.S. borders.

According to newly released Project STEALTH documentation, over half of the world's active ninjas belong to a very powerful *Tamatama Ryu*. Despite over 20 years of intelligence gathering, Project Stealth has never identified the *jonin* of the *Tamatama Ryu*. Speculation has been wild, with everyone from Osama bin Laden, Dick Cheney to Tupac Shakur named the suspected leader. One thing *is* known, however: *Tamatama*'s chief is the world's most powerful living human.

Another laughable and deadly myth about ninjas is that they're primarily Japanese males. In fact, the ninja comes in all shapes, sizes and colors. The ninja art has spread across all six inhabited continents, and has attracted practitioners from over 100 countries. While most ninjas are thin, muscular and physically fit, there have been a few recorded cases of successful, clinically obese ninjas—adding to the cold fact that there is no sure-fire way to recognize a ninja assassin.

Ninjas are more prevalent in the world today than ever before. When Japan closed its doors to foreign influence in the mid-1600s, ninja operations were limited to the Japanese islands, the Korean peninsula and a swath of eastern China. Today, the "Ninja Problem" is considered a global scourge with an estimated 20,000 to 200,000 ninjas operating at any given time around the globe.

CHAPTER 2

KNOW THE NINJA

Understanding the tactics, mindset and abilities of the ninja are the keys to avoiding and repelling a ninja attack. Take a bit of time to try to wrap your head around *who* your ninja assassin is, and *how* he or she might go about killing you.

✳ ✳ ✳

NINJAS AND THEIR TWENTY-SOME SENSES

Most people are familiar with the basic human "five senses." Neurobiologists believe humans actually possess no fewer than ten. An anomaly of science, the ninja is known to employ up to 20. Take note: A sense of humor is not included.

PRIMARY SENSES

The following are the ten basic human senses used daily (the first five are the Aristotelian Five):

- **Sight**, the ability to see shapes, colors and blood.
- **Hearing**, the ability to audibly sense the swish of a ninja sword.
- **Touch**, the ability to feel the cold ground beneath your face.

- **Smell**, the ability to inhale and detect the scent of your own sweat.
- **Taste**, the ability to sense the subtle flavor of adrenaline.
- **Nociception**, the ability to sense the pain of an imbedded *shuriken*.
- **Equilibrioception**, the ability to remain balanced while standing on a small post.
- **Proprioception and kinesthesia**, the ability to control joint motion and acceleration when running for your life.
- **Sense of time**, the ability not to show up late to a fight (or your own death).
- **Thermoception**, the ability to sense a cool breeze brought on by a swiftly moving ninja.

DIMINISHED VESTIGIAL AND MUTATED SENSES

The following senses are weak or non-existent in almost all humans. However, neurobiologists believe that about 1/400,000 humans possess significant "sixth-sense" abilities. For ninjas, that statistic goes up to 97/100.

- **Magnetoception**, the sense of magnetic North. This perception is generally strong in migratory birds and ninjas, both of whom possess "an impeccable sense of direction."
- **Electroception**, the ability to pick up changes in subtle electric charges, like the rapid beating of a terrified victim's heart.
- **Echolocation**, the ability to determine distance through sound. Ninjas use this sense to navigate through your darkened bedroom.
- **Night vision**, the ability to see at night. Night vision is employed by cats, snakes and ninjas, who enjoy hunting after sundown.
- **Telepathy**, the ability to read the thoughts of other beings. A ninja is doing this to you. Right now.

- ❋ **Clairvoyance**, the ability to anticipate the location or movement of objects without use of the five senses. Ninjas call this "basic preparation."
- ❋ **Precognition/Retrocognition**, the ability to ascertain information about the future or the past without physical information—ninjas consider this the "lazy man's recon."
- ❋ **Psychokinesis**, the ability to transport blades into abdomens without physical exertion, using the mind alone.
- ❋ **Pyrokinesis**, one of the ninja's favorite tools, the ability to create and control fire with the mind.

NINJA ADOPTION

Although rare, every once in a while non-ninjas are recruited to join a *ryu* due to a favorable genetic anomaly such as an acute vestigial or mutated sense. Once recruited, these "adopted ninjas" are treated as equals.

THE DARK ABILITIES OF THE NINJA

Aside from their heightened senses and physical agility, ninjas put a lot of emphasis on how they collect intel and prepare and execute an attack without ever being seen.

INFILTRATION

The ability to infiltrate an enemy's stronghold is as important to ninjas as their combat skills. The ninja, in addition to being one of the world's deadliest assassins, is also one of the world's most capable spies.

NINJA INVISIBILITY

For the ninja, remaining "invisible" may mean any number of things. Most people hear "ninja invisibility" and immediately picture a ninja shrouded in a dark *shinobi-shozoku* (traditional black outfit), slipping quietly through shadows. While ninjas often do employ various tactics to remain unperceived, they may also employ any number of skills to remain invisible in broad daylight. For the ninja, remaining "invisible" can simply mean not revealing that he or she is, in fact, a ninja.

Going Unperceived

The ninja often navigates our world enshrouded in a fog of impermeable darkness—undetectable by even the most attentive observer. Going unperceived does not just mean going unseen, but also going unheard, un-smelt, unfelt and un-tasted.

1. Invisible Movement: Ninjas begin training in the art of "invisible movement" at birth—specifically focused in the game hide-seek-and-kill. As ninjas grow older, they incorporate specific techniques into their invisibility arsenal. Many forms of walking are learned to prevent detection, including sideways "crab walking," dense-underbrush "silent-stab-and-step strolling" as well as a "slow, aimless meandering." The traditional black outfits donned at night—*shinobi-shozoku*—are traded for snow-white winter garb for white-out conditions, urban gray for city assaults and evening-chic for more formal attacks.

2. Camouflaged Invisibility: In addition to invisibility techniques, the ninja employs a remarkable capacity for camouflage as inanimate objects. In fact, the ninja's abilities are so strong that, according to statistics, at any given time there is a disguised ninja within 20 yards of you. Remember that potted plant that one day disappeared? Ninja. That brick wall covered in "graffiti" you pass on your way to work? Ninja. The soft, comfortable chair you're sitting in? You get the point.

3. Scentlessness: Ninjas will alter their smell depending on their task. This is especially important when a target has employed a watch-dog or watch-tiger. Ninjas will cover their scent by rubbing themselves with whatever best blends in with the environment—pine cones, car exhaust, Chanel, manure, etc. Furthermore, ninjas will also be careful to remain upwind from the target whenever possible.

4. Touchlessness: Ninjas pass through the night like a gentle Eastern wind. When moving, ninjas will not stir the air, shake the ground nor do anything else that will allow you to feel their movement. You will not *feel* the ninja until the ninja's cold blade touches you.

Disguise and Appearance Alteration

In addition to being trained killers, ninjas are also Daytime Emmy–worthy actors, wearing whatever "mask" is required to remain undercover. Historically in feudal Japan, ninjas employed seven disguises—entertainer, musician, merchant, nomadic priest, Buddhist monk, mountain warrior or *ronin* samurai. The female ninja, or *kunoichi* (see page 40), employed her own impressive set of disguises. Today, ninjas have learned to adapt to a diverse and complex world of people.

Skilled ninjas will go to great lengths to alter their appearance very quickly, using fake beards, glasses, wigs, fat suits, etc. A young male ninja can transform himself into a fat elderly woman in less than ten minutes. The following is just a smattering of some of the ninja's "fall-back" disguises.

1. Bum: In larger cities ninjas may disguise themselves as homeless beggars. Commonly avoided and ignored by most citizens, this disguise allows ninjas to easily observe and track their victims while making a bit of loose change.

2. Country Hick: Similar to the rednecks of America's heartland, the "country bumpkin" is a near-universal character and a disguise easily replicated by ninjas. If you're in a large city, these shabby-clothed farm-hand ninjas are easy to spot and usually means the ninja is a novice who lacks cultural understanding. No matter where you are in the world, keep an eye out for misplaced hillbillies.

3. Taxi Driver: Also used in larger cities and especially prevalent in the world's mega-metropolises, the taxi driver disguise is one of the ninja's favorites as it allows for the most diversity and creativity. As taxi drivers, ninjas will assume the appearance, accent, personality, body odor and historical and political narrative of their assigned characters.

4. Musician: This is perhaps the hardest disguise for ninjas to pull off. Because ninjas spend most of their time training, they have little opportunity for recreational activities such as learning an instrument. As such, ALL NINJAS ARE TERRIBLE MUSICIANS. If a ninja is disguised as a musician, it will either be as a poor karaoke singer, a humorous singer/songwriter, or as someone who carries an instrument but never *plays* it.

5. Construction Worker/Fireman/Police Officer/Indian/Etc.: The popular '70s disco group The Village People was based off a 1960s ninja clan that donned similar disguises during the notorious Greenwich Village Ninja Strike of January 1968 that claimed the lives of two dozen hippies. Today, ninjas disguised as public workers will wear more authentic costumes than they once did. These disguises can be particularly dangerous; if you suspect you're being followed by a ninja, or think a ninja attack is imminent, your first instinct will be to call the police. However, the "policeman" who shows up at your house may be the very ninja who had been following you!

6. Girl Scout: Young-looking pygmy ninjas will dress up as Girl Scouts selling cookies door to door. If you hear your doorbell ring and find a strange-looking Girl Scout standing on your stoop, purchase a few boxes but DO NOT EAT THEM.

7. Flirtatious Intern: Contrary to popular conception, ninjas do have sexual desires—deadly strong ones. Thus, playing the part of the flirtatious intern is particularly desirable for many ninjas vying for assignments. Be cautious of any new interns you may have at work; this is the primary reason office romances are frowned upon by management.

8. New Best Friend: If a ninja has been assigned to perform prolonged espionage on you, he or she will often attempt to befriend you. With a superior understanding of the Five Weaknesses (see page 38), the ninja can easily gain the trust of most lonely people. Avoid making friends.

9) The "Old Lady" Who Needs Help Crossing the Street: Have you ever *really* seen an old lady trying to cross a street? Mull that over a bit.

MURDER ON THE STRIP

The tourism slogan "What happens in Vegas, stays in Vegas" was originally adopted from an article in the *Las Vegas Star Journal*. Apparently, what "happens in Vegas" is violent ninja attacks; what "stays in Vegas" are the severed parts of the dead bodies.

CONFUSION TECHNIQUES

Ninjas are like calculus.

—*Saul Ribero, intelligence analyst, Project STEALTH*

What do calculus and ninjas have in common? Everything. Just like calculus, the ninja is impossible to figure out, understood only by an elite few and generally feared by the masses. Instilling this horrendous mixture of fear and confusion in an opponent is key to the ninjas' success. And at that, they are MIT professors.

- **Visual Distractions (Smoke Bombs):** The most well-known visual distraction employed by ninjas is the smoke bomb, allowing them to travel and attack unseen.

- **Bird Songs/Animal Noises:** Ninjas can mimic the sounds, songs and calls of a variety of animals. While you're looking for the rare cockatiel or trying to locate the mating sea turtles, your ninja assassin will employ a swift and efficient strike.

- **Optical Illusion:** Never trust your depth perception when it comes to ninjas. Ninjas in real life are always closer than they appear.

- **Riddles:** The ninja may ask you a particularly difficult yet engaging riddle. Unfortunately, the answer inherently includes "your death" somewhere.

To enter this world
Naked a blessing, leaving
it nude, a dire curse
— *Ancient Haiku, Anon.*

THE NINJA VENTRILOQUIST ON THE MANHATTAN 6 TRAIN

I was riding on the 6 train in Manhattan when suddenly somebody started shouting really disgusting, perverted things like "I wanna sex you up," "I like big butts and I cannot lie" and "I really dig Lady Gaga!" There were several young women on the train and they became very uncomfortable. I looked around to see who was saying such terrible things, when I realized the girls were all glaring at me! When I got to work, I told my boss about what had happened. He smiled and said, "Just a ninja ventriloquist looking for a little fun. Fortunately for you, it was only practice."

—*Intern #48, Project STEALTH*

MIND MANIPULATION

Undergoing ninja mind manipulation is like being waterboarded from the inside out.

    —*Lt. Rodwell Johnston, U.S. Navy SEAL*

For centuries, people in the West have neglected mental development, buying into the myth that a "ripped" or "sexy" body is the way to success. Western media perpetuates the notion that mind and body are two entities separated by a schism. Most diets and workout regimens encourage developing the body apart from the mind, which we tend to leave for academics to cultivate. But where ninjas are concerned, the separation of mind and body and the resulting lack of mental discipline is the Western world's fatal flaw. Mind (over matter) is the ninja's most powerful weapon.

Learning mind manipulation tactics is the final phase of *ninjutsu* training and the penultimate step toward manipulating the universe. Ninjas have a psychological capacity surpassing those of highly trained hypnotists and military psy-ops specialists. Ninjas can coerce or persuade their victim, leading to an attack that appears to be no attack at all. Mind manipulation works most effectively when the target does not realize he or she has been hit.

Manipulation may come in the guise of romance. Your significant other may be a ninja who has meticulously targeted and re-created your likes, desires and preferences to create the illusion of a viable love interest. When you least expect it—*pow!*—poison dart to the neck. Female ninja double agents are most often employed against male targets because men's ego-centered conviction that they're irresistible to women leaves them vulnerable to such deceptions.

The "significant other" threat shows how the mind manipulations of the ninja work on a small scale. Similar, though perhaps less sophisticated, psychological operations, or "psy-ops" for short, have been, and continue to be, the backbone of intelligence operations around the world, from the CIA to the United Kingdom's MI6. All are based on ninja techniques and tactics.

BEAUTIFUL BUXOM BLONDE AT THE BAR FIND YOU APPEALING?

Not so fast. *Evaluate:* Does this normally happen? *Determine:* No, it doesn't; this doesn't feel right. *Escape:* This is a ninja. Cover your mouth, act sick, make for the door . . . . Close call!

The Five Weaknesses are points of psychological manipulation that the trained ninja will use to throw you off your game or even persuade you to throw yourself off a bridge. This way, the ninja can harm you without your realizing that you're a target and sometimes without ever laying a hand on you. Terrifying, yes. Unstoppable, no.

The Five Weaknesses

For centuries ninjas have studied the human mind and searched for exploitable weaknesses. They have identified the five main exploitable human weaknesses—anger, sympathy, greed, fear and lust. They're associated with the five elements: earth (*chi*), air (*fu*), fire (*la*), water (*sui*) and void (*ku*). Knowing how to use these emotions is key to the ninja's success in mind manipulation and espionage. Controlling your own mind and guarding against these Five Weaknesses is your best hope for surviving a ninja strike.

Anger

Whether it's getting cut off by a Hummer on your morning commute, having hot coffee spilled on your new laptop by a clumsy waiter or finding your girlfriend in bed with your boss the day after you get laid off, anger is all too common and easily unleashed. It clouds your judgment and forces irrational behavior with little regard for personal safety. A ninja can use your anger against you with remarkable ease.

Make every effort to avoid anger. Practice meditation, yoga or tai chi. Stop drinking coffee and playing video games. Get plenty of exercise and at least eight hours of sleep every night. If you live with your mother, move out. Above all, relax and breathe.

Sympathy

Sympathy, the emotion associated with earth, is unlike the other Five Weaknesses in that it's both a strength and weakness. A little sympathy can make you a better friend, lover, brother or mother. Too much of it, however, makes you vulnerable to manipulation and dupery.

When it comes to ninja attacks, the altruistic victim may fall for the simplest of setups—helping an old woman (who is actually a ninja in disguise) across the street and getting hit by a car while she sprints out of the way.

Greed

Greed, as we know it today, usually involves the accumulation of earthly goods, from cold, hard cash to property like cars, televisions and toy poodles. Unfortunately for those who are looking to accumulate wealth without effort, straddling the top of every pyramid scheme is a ninja.

Fear

Fear, one of the most fundamental emotions and the basis for the "flight" part of the "fight-or-flight" response, is an easy emotion for ninjas to target. We experience a similar fear reaction when presented with potential danger or the illusion of danger that comes with a superstition or a phobia we do not understand. For example, people who are terrified of ghosts, arachnids, immigrants or carbohydrates experience the same biological responses as a person being held at gunpoint in a dark alley.

A ninja's attempts to manipulate his victim's fear—for example, by filling the victim's apartment with aliens—may be effective, but they can also be costly for the ninja. Instead, the ninja will attempt to get close to his victim and learn his fears and anxieties, then create a false bond of companionship and confidence between himself and the victim. In this role, the ninja can subtly and constantly instill paranoia.

Lust

Lust is the overwhelming and uncontrollable desire for sex. Unlike the other four weaknesses, uncontrolled lust can make the victim a participant in his or her own demise. There is truly nothing more degrading than to be assassinated while naked.

Lust is perhaps the most insidious of the Five Weaknesses, because the lustful victim is the easiest to trick, dupe or coerce. The proliferation of black widows in popular culture and the suspicious, sexy femme fatales in film noir reveal Hollywood's obsession with the concept of sexuality as vulnerability. Tricking a lustful man to his destruction is a tale as old as storytelling itself.

Female ninjas, known as *kunoichi*, are specially trained to fulfill the role of seductress. Male ninjas, with their svelte, muscular bodies, mysterious dark personas and remarkable flexibility and stamina, are equally adept at sexy evil.

If you have reason to believe a ninja attack may be on the way, take precautions against your erotic impulses. Above all, remain celibate. Refrain from entering into any new relationships. Take cold showers and take care of your own needs. Or join a monastery.

Tactics of Prevention

Protecting yourself against mind manipulation is not an easy feat, but by understanding the Five Weaknesses you can start to purify your body and mind. Actively guard your mind against manipulation. Consider following the same kind of diet and mind training that the ninjas use.

Go to the library and check out some books on CIA interrogation techniques, covert operations and espionage. They may help give you a more well-rounded understanding of mind manipulation techniques. Reading these books may also instill fear and paranoia, encouraging you to clear your mind and life of potential distractions. Just as ninjas learn to clear their mind, so too must you if you hope to survive the deadliest attack of all—mind manipulation.

FEMALE NINJAS (KUNOICHI)

Despite common feminist assumptions, the female ninja (or *kunoichi* in Japanese) is trained differently from her male counterparts. But don't be fooled—the female ninja is just as deadly as her male counterparts, though she will readily exploit stereotypes of feminine weakness to her advantage. Female ninjas are traditionally trained in the use of

small concealed weapons, disguises and poisons, as well as using their bosomy sexuality to their advantage. Women in both feudal Japan and modern society have been consistently underestimated, giving them an incredible advantage, particularly when it comes to espionage.

CONCEALED WEAPONS AND POISONS

Kunoichi are trained to wield much smaller weapons than male ninjas, choosing a dagger, small blade or throwing star instead of a sword or wooden staff. The smaller weapons allow the *kunoichi* to successfully conceal their implement of death in the sleeve of a kimono, a pair of butt-tight jeans or an absurdly small handbag.

CURRENT FASHION TRENDS

Today's "layered" look has proven very beneficial to *kunoichi*. With "skin-tight" out and looser, longer clothing in, the female ninja has more places to hide weapons without resorting to "extreme measures."

According to Project STEALTH research, female ninjas have also traditionally used props to conceal their weapons. In the past, a female ninja might use a cat or bouquet of flowers to conceal her poisoned dart or dagger. Today, small yappy dogs or Fendi bags can serve a similar purpose. Be especially aware of women carrying small, yappy dogs *in* Fendi bags.

Besides traditional concealed weapons, female ninjas are trained to turn even the most mundane household items into deadly weapons. A bobby pin may be tipped with poison. Eyebrow tweezers can become a dagger.

DISGUISE

The female ninja is trained in the arts of disguise. Back in the day, *kunoichi* chose to disguise themselves as prostitutes, geishas, entertainers, household servants or even cooks. These disguises enabled her to become close to her intended target, and obtain secret and personal information about daily routines, medications and intimate desires.

Today, female ninjas will maintain less obtrusive cover, choosing instead to take a position as a barista at your favorite coffee shop, a new coworker at your job or the uber-flexible pilates instructor at your gym. Before you know it, you're Facebook friends with this new and exciting girl. Maybe you exchange e-mail addresses, begin to Gchat. You begin to warm to her. And she starts to get to know you.

CHAPTER 3

DETECTING A NINJA

Ninjas, more than terrorism, flu pandemics, economic failure or climate change, are America's biggest threat today.
—*Henrich S. Mjolner, co-creator and under-secretary, Project STEALTH*

✳ ✳ ✳

This chapter covers the most common spots you might encounter ninjas in your day-to-day life, from classic hiding places like treetops and alleyways to less-expected locations such as bathtubs, pantries and telephone wires. Furthermore, the information provides guidelines for detecting ninjas yourself, no matter what the location. This list is by no means exhaustive, nor does it cover every place where you might find a ninja. After all, ninjas are tricksters, neither mechanical nor predictable. These lethal killing machines are not robots, zombies or elite military forces. They're ninjas, the world's foremost assassins and spies. Once you accept that fact, your eyes will open for the first time, and you'll see ninjas everywhere.

IMMEDIATELY OUTSIDE YOUR HOME

It's important to look at the outside world the way a caveman would in the bear-infested Stone Age. As you exit the relative safety of your hovel, prepare for and expect the worst.

TREETOPS

Treetops are the quintessential ninja hideaway, according to countless works of ninja literature and cinema. The canopy-shrouded upper branches of a tree provide ninjas with an unrivaled vantage point out of the average pedestrian's line of sight. Most often, ninjas prefer trees with dense foliage. In the United States, these include maple, palm, oak and even the towering redwood. Trees with extensive foliage help obscure the ninja's body, wrapping it in a delicate and shimmering shadow. If no leafy trees are available, ninjas are likely to choose bald or dead trees with beefy branches that can support their entire body weight. They'll wrap their bodies snakelike around a branch, becoming just another knot in the bough.

Wearing traditional *jika-tabi* footwear along with *aishiki* (shoe spikes) on their feet and *shuku* ("tiger claws") on their hands, ninjas can scurry up all varieties of trees. Once they're at the top, they use their extraordinary leg strength and agility to jump from tree to tree, only slightly disturbing the canopy and nut-fetching rodents. A ninja's treetop travel mimics the sound of a slight wind rustling the branches.

Remember, trees are just as likely to be used as hiding places in the big city as in rural areas. Even in neighborhoods where foliage is sparse, ninjas may still make a home in shrubbery or young saplings.

Scouring the trees for the silhouette of a ninja is pointless. Chances are you won't be able to spot him or her. Instead, focus on searching for movement among the branches. Employ powerful binoculars to scan the trees directly outside your home or office. To avoid getting arrested for perverse behavior, keep a copy of *The Compendium of North American Birds* in your binocular case.

Spotting a ninja in a tree may be confusing. They may be dressed not in traditional loose black clothing but rather in neutral-hued spandex or camouflage-colored lightweight cotton. Both provide ease of movement, comfort and a covert "tree-hugger" look.

If you find a ninja perched in a treetop in your neighborhood, consider taking a lengthy vacation in hopes he or she will get hungry and leave. Climbing a nearby tree to spy on or shout at the ninja is a very bad idea. If you must take action, call your local fire department and notify them of a "large black cat" stuck in a tree. The commotion will likely cause the ninja to flee.

ALERTING THE AUTHORITIES

Never call 911 and inform the dispatcher that you've spotted a "ninja who may be trying to kill me." You'll end up under forced 24-hour psychiatric evaluation—the perfect locale and opportunity for a lethal ninja attack.

If the ninja temporarily abandons his or her treetop post, take the opportunity to hire a tree trimmer. This is also your chance to plan, read the rest of this guide and try to figure out why the ninja is conducting reconnaissance on *you*.

TELEPHONE POLES, LAMPPOSTS AND WIRES

Telephone poles and lampposts, the modern urban incarnations of tall trees, are favorite ninja hiding spots in the big city. Like their natural leafy counterparts, these poles are easily scaled by the agile ninja with hand and foot claws. In moments of conspicuous ascent, ninjas may pose as phone or city maintenance crew to make their way up in a less stealthy manner.

CABLE AND TELEPHONE REPAIR

Trust nobody who claims they need to work on power lines, TV/internet cables or telephone wires. Their shifty, unpunctual nature is purposefully obnoxious and distracting.

Besides being adept climbers, ninjas are expert tightrope walkers. They can meander across telephone lines with the ease and grace of a squirrel. The ninja you thought you saw a second ago may be well down the block by now.

As a precaution, consider moving to an apartment or house where your windows are not accessible via telephone lines. Many cities have put their telephone lines underground in response to the perpetual ninja threat. Yet, at present, proximity to telephone lines remains a serious factor to consider when protecting yourself and your family against ninjas. Lobby your local city government to bury all wires and cables.

DARK ALLEYWAYS

Muggers, thugs, vagabonds, rats, roaches, garbage and ninjas are all found in the dark recesses of urban alleyways. When strolling down an eerily silent alley, casually check behind dumpsters and scan overhead fire escapes for crouching ninjas. Dark alleyways may seem more ominous at night, but remember, a ninja will strike at any time, day or night.

Consider the average alleyway a kind of seedy Thermopylae. Battling in an alley is narrow and difficult. The ninja, like the Spartans before them, know how to take advantage of the funneling effect, making your escape much harder. If you have to enter an alleyway with more than one person, always travel single file, at least 28 paces apart, to avoid a lethal bottleneck.

THE SOUNDS OF SILENCE

You won't hear the pitter-patter of little ninja feet, so don't listen for them. Audible footsteps behind you are a sign that you're safe from a ninja attack, at least for now. If an alleyway is completely silent, don't walk into it. Listen for the reassuring soft moans and whispers of human life before entering.

In an alleyway you've never taken before, if you think you glimpse a ninja out of the corner of your eye, keep on walking as if you haven't seen a thing. Chances are this ninja is not laying in wait for you, or you wouldn't see him or her at all.

YOUR VEHICLE

No matter what type of car you drive or how well you drive it, your vehicle will always be a prime target for ninja attacks. Take special precaution when entering, exiting and operating your motor vehicle.

CAR TRUNKS

In the past five years alone, there have been over 200 reports of ninjas hiding in the trunks of their victim's cars—especially open-compartment SUVs and station wagons. Hiding in your car for an extended period of time, especially in the trunk, allows the ninja to get a sense of your daily routine and figure out the least conspicuous place for an attack.

One way to avoid winding up with a ninja in your trunk is to always keep it full of clutter such as bubble wrap, tin foil, pebbles or eggshells—items that make enough noise to warn you when something is amiss. Clever anti-ninja operatives often cram their entire cars, except for the driver's seat, with "stuff," essentially ninja-proofing their vehicles.

ANTI-NINJA "HOTBOX"

The inside temperature of parked cars can rise to upward of 140 degrees Fahrenheit in summer. The baking, potentially deadly heat is a prime deterrent against lurking ninjas. During summer months, create a "hotbox" by parking in direct sunlight with the windows tightly sealed. Remember to take your dog or baby with you when you leave the vehicle.

GARAGES AND PARKING LOTS

Cluttered home garages are not only easy places to hide but prime locations for attacks. There may be household tools such as rakes, hoses, axes and plows the ninja can use in an impromptu attack. Clear your garage as much as possible, shoving what remains into tight spaces. Develop a keen sense of sight and a sense of your own space. You may want to photograph the garage and its contents, keeping the photos in your wallet for quick review if you suspect a ninja may be lurking.

Avoid public garages at all costs. The quiet, multi-leveled structures give ninjas plenty of hiding spots and leave you with few defenses and escape routes. Always park on the street or in open parking lots where visibility is increased.

INSIDE YOUR HOUSE

A home incursion is often described as the most horrific and violating event one can experience. The unfortunate fact is, when it comes to ninjas, this violation of space *has* happened and *will* happen again.

Knowing where a ninja may be concealed will give you peace of mind today and potentially save your life tomorrow.

ENTRYWAY

Doorways, rafters and indoor industrial piping provide perfect hiding spots for a ninja who has entered your house. When you open your front door, quickly scan the ceiling and beams, prepared for a sudden ninja strike.

Hiding spots above the average person's eye level have proven to be the most successful places from which to launch a ninja attack. Most people, arriving home drained of energy and even mentally brutalized from their day at the office, tend to look down and shuffle through copious amounts of junk mail.

Perching directly above doorways is one of the most athletic and effective positions a ninja will take. Straddling the top of the doorway, precisely balanced on the narrowest of trim, allows the ninja to spring elegantly onto an unsuspecting victim.

The best way to enter your foyer or front hallway is always at top speed. Once you've unlocked the door, kick it open and bolt through your house or apartment to a designated safe room.

LIVING ROOM

The living room is full of good hiding places for the ninja to lay in wait. They can hide beneath the couch, behind the curtains, on the windowsill or under the coffee table. Be especially wary of "fort-building" ninjas that can create a deadly mess.

THAT AIN'T SANTA CLAUS

The only person you're likely to ever find descending your soot-covered chimney is a ninja assassin.

DINING ROOM

The dining room, often sparsely decorated, is an unlikely place to find a hiding ninja. However, if you enjoy food, the ninja may choose to attack after a particularly engorging meal. Always check the underside of your dining table. Be careful of any meal served on a closed silver platter, as infant ninjas are often hidden inside.

DEN

The den, like the living room, offers a plethora of places for the ninja to hide—bulky, old-school television sets, fully stocked bars and or foosball tables are especially dangerous locales.

Because a successful escape requires parachuting from 30,000 feet, which many ninjas find annoyingly chilly, ninjas rarely attack on jetliners. As long as you stay in plain sight and don't use the lavatory or stroll to the back of the plane, where an impromptu attack could take place, you can relax and enjoy the "friendly" skies.

KITCHEN

A favorite activity of the ninja is to lie in wait in a target's kitchen as it gives the ninja a chance to enjoy a snack or a full meal without straying too far from his or her concealed position. When entering your kitchen, violently open all cabinet, refrigerator and dishwasher doors.

LAUNDRY FACILITY

Ninjas often make use of vacant washing machines and dryers for surprise attacks. Always turn laundry machines on before you open the doors. Listen for the distinctive *thud-clunk-thud* of a revolving human body.

BEDROOM

Bedrooms are extremely dangerous places because of their primary purpose—sleep. A ninja hiding in your mattress or box spring need only thrust a blade through the soft bedding to impale you mid-snooze. Always look under your bed and mattress before going to sleep. Of course, the smartest idea is to use a sleeping bag and bedroll instead of a full bed. Check the sleeping bag for common booby traps like poisonous snakes, spiders and scorpions.

Avoid using closets and dressers. Reduce your wardrobe to seven to ten items and keep them neatly folded in a corner of your room.

BATHROOM

The bathroom is a prime spot for a ninja attack. The dangers of a closed, opaque shower curtain, an explosive-laden toilet seat or poisoned toiletries make the bathroom a place to be feared, not enjoyed.

The bathtub, a place for relaxation and romantically scented bubbles, can also be a deathtrap. Never sit idle in a hot bath. A soak does not help you survive. When you run a bath or turn on the shower, check the water with a pH strip to make sure it has not been chemically altered.

Empty bathtubs offer excellent hiding places for ninjas capable of blending in with smooth, curved porcelain. Deny the space by filling your bath with dirt and indoor plants. If you intend to keep your tub, you might also consider applying slow-drying roof tar to the bottom of the tub every morning. That way, a ninja might find him or herself unexpectedly stuck to the bottom surface.

Do not use toothpaste. It is easily poisoned. If you must use a toothbrush, carry it with you, preferably around your neck, for safekeeping.

Set up a complex system of mirrors so you can check all areas of the bathroom from a distance. You might even install a camera that streams video to your cell phone. This may help you detect a ninja and also deters ninjas from hiding in your bathtub at all.

ON THE GO

Traveling between any two points leaves you vulnerable for an extended period of time. Always prepare and draw out how you're going to move and what you need to do if disaster strikes.

ROADWAYS

When driving on surface streets, be on the lookout for possible ninja hiding places, especially when at stops. The ninja may crouch in a roadside ditch or hide behind a billboard or flanking shrubbery. Remember, ninjas can conceal themselves behind lamp poles and sign posts that are less than four inches wide.

FREEWAYS

A ninja attack is unlikely on a freeway when traffic is moving at a brisk pace. However, ninjas are known to cause traffic-halting fender benders and full-on pile-ups to facilitate an attack. If you see an accident, DO NOT STOP or rubberneck. If you're in an accident yourself, your best bet is to GET OUT OF YOUR CAR IMMEDIATELY AND RUN. A hefty fine and bit of jail time is better than a ninja sword in your abdomen.

TUNNELS AND BRIDGES

Bridges and tunnels compress traffic into confined, inescapable spaces. Expect a ninja assassin to take full advantage of these situations. If you commute over a body of water or through a tunnel, take extreme caution and avoid the route whenever possible.

Despite the toxic fumes, tunnels offer dark hiding places for prowling ninjas. They also provide ideal ninja shelters from rain, snow, hail and freak tornadoes.

Bridges, especially those with Art Deco flourishes or vaulting supports, allow ninjas to travel high above traffic and wait patiently with pleasing views of the surrounding landscape.

Attacks in tunnels or under bridges come from above. Ninjas may land on car roofs or in truck beds. If you regularly travel through tunnels or cross bridges on your way to work, remove any roof racks from your vehicle and avoid driving a pickup or convertible that is especially susceptible to ninja assault. Avoid driving roadways with tunnels or bridges in heavy traffic.

If you anticipate a bridge or tunnel attack, whatever you do, don't stop moving. Slamming on the brakes or otherwise halting your car gives ninjas a chance to leap into action. Keep driving straight, accelerating to match the flow of traffic and passing slower cars if possible. When you reach a street with lateral exit routes, steer your vehicle to the roadside and begin evasive maneuvers.

When approaching a tunnel or bridge, or during an attack, drive erratically. Avoid conventional rules of the road. Ninjas are trained to attack in the context of predictable situations. Driving like a "bat out of hell" may force them to resort to dangerous improvisations.

If a ninja attack is underway, try to eliminate the threat by speeding up, hitting the brakes and accelerating again. Swerve side to side while screaming. Put your hazard lights on to alert other motorists of the attack. Be aware, though, that ninjas are very hard to shake. Erratic driving, however, may force the ninja to hold on for dear life, limiting the opportunity for a violent attack.

GAS STATIONS

Late at night, unattended gas stations are ninja havens. Keep an eye on nearby garbage cans, parked cars, overhangs, awnings and wandering hookers. Night attendants working behind bulletproof glass are a definite sign that ninja attacks have occurred there before.

PUBLIC TRANSPORTATION

Subway systems, such as BART in the San Francisco Bay Area, the MTA in New York City, the T in Boston and the Metro in Washington, DC, account for a staggering percentage of ninja attack sites in the U.S. If you fear that you might be a ninja target, avoid public transportation altogether.

If you choose to take the risk and continue to ride public transit, follow these rules strictly:

- Wear enough clothing to conceal your entire body. A hood, gloves, baseball cap and shifty mask should suffice.
- Take a train/bus in the *opposite* direction of your intended destination. Switch to the proper line four stops later.

- Change seats/cars at every single stop.
- Pay in exact change.
- Carry an empty, large, cumbersome case with the words "guns & ammo" emblazoned on the side.
- Mutter words like "ninja" and "attack" to yourself and those around you. If ninjas suspect you're on to them, they'll postpone their attack.
- Pretend to listen to an iPod and nod to a fake beat, but stay extremely vigilant.
- Dart your eyes around the train or bus constantly. Not only will you be more observant, you'll also look slightly dangerous/crazy.

Avoid taxis, shuttle buses and other transportation modes in which you're at the mercy of another driver—especially in foreign countries where cab drivers are easily bribed to take victims to a predetermined attack location. All cab drivers should be considered suspect (see page 33).

When traveling on long-distance Amtrak trains, be as vigilant and visible as possible at all times. Never book a private compartment. Instead, stay in the dining car or club car for the whole trip. Keep buying food items to avoid seeming suspicious, but to prevent being poisoned, don't eat anything. If a conductor questions your six-hour lunch, just say, "Trains disrupt my metabolism, so I have to consume as many salty snacks as possible." Pretend to nibble on something until they leave. Do not doze off. Do not listen to music or read a book. Maintain an attentive, interested look as though you'd just heard a witty anecdote.

Most passengers prefer to travel inside the train, but ninjas travel on top of it. Keep a sharp ear out for any movement on the car roof above you. Inform an attendant or conductor if you suspect anything unusual.

AIRPLANES

Ninjas rarely board commercial jetliners because of the security checks. But when one of them does use their stealth training to slither through a checkpoint as the TSA agents are looking the other way, it can lead to a frightening, even deadly, in-flight ninja attack. Very few attacks come midflight. Instead, the ninja stows away in a cargo hold, disguised as luggage, only to surprise you as you wait bleary eyed at the baggage claim area after arrival.

BORDER ATTACKS

The U.S. Department of Homeland Security is trying to halt illegal ninjagration with sturdier border walls and barricades, but these measures have not quelled the violence that the ninjas secretly provoke. In 2008 and 2009, a ferocious upswing in violence in Mexico's northern border regions was caused by just two ninja teams. That said, never approach a border patrol checkpoint. These congested areas allow for "strike and split" attacks, in which the ninja assailant hits you in one country before disappearing into the other.

BE VIGILANT

This list of places to look for ninjas is neither exhaustive nor all-inclusive. You might find a ninja hiding in your kitchen cabinet, in the pantry, under the bed or any myriad places not mentioned in this chapter. At least now, armed with an idea of what to look for and where to look first, you can significantly reduce your chances of being murdered in a ninja attack.

CHAPTER 4

DEFENDING AGAINST A NINJA ATTACK

To this day I can't believe I survived! I was fat and obnoxious. I was addicted to cigarettes, alcohol and adultery. I had lived a hard, fast life and left a trail of enemies. While I was divorcing my third wife, I became a chronic gambler and began picking fights with strangers. I knew there was a good chance that one of the people I had pissed off would hire someone to take revenge, so I started preparing for the inevitable. I assassin-proofed my house and body in every possible way. I trained myself to sleep lightly and took intense self-defense classes. When the attack came, I thought it would be a hit man. I was prepared. I didn't think it would possibly be a ninja, but it was. The assault was horrific. It left me with a broken back, four deep stab wounds and a cracked skull, to name the worst of it. But I survived. I managed to fend off one of the planet's best killers. Am I still paranoid? Of course I am. But I've turned my life around. And I'll always be prepared. It was paranoia alone that saved my life.

—*"Jeremy," ninja attack survivor*

✳ ✳ ✳

Most people, hearing Jeremy's story, conclude that his preparation was fueled by extreme paranoia. In reality, the only thing abnormal about Jeremy's experience is the fact that he survived. In the last decade, fewer than two percent of all ninja targets have lived to tell about the attack. In almost all these cases, the survivors were highly trained individuals such as elite military Special Forces, or else they died from their injuries shortly after being attacked.

EXERCISES IN FUTILITY

Posing the question "Why is a ninja attacking me?" is, paradoxically, a fantastic thing to ask yourself *before* the ninja attack begins. Chances are you've done something to deserve this ninja attack. The ninja has been hired by someone who knows you, perhaps even loves you. Do not, however, dwell on *why* the ninja is attacking you. It won't help.

In addition, prayer almost never helps in defending against a ninja attack. In fact, prayers can facilitate the attack. Besides immobilizing the victim, here are three reasons that prayer is futile against a ninja:

- God (assuming He/She/It exists) is busy. Even if God does decide to intervene, it'll take time for God to turn His/Her/Its attention to your predicament. Ninjas are swift and will attack before you've received divine intervention.
- If you do not believe in God, He/She/It will have no reason to save you.
- A ninja's breath is considered a blessing and a prayer. Therefore, your ninja assassin is outpraying you by about 10,000 to 1. Which one of you, do you think, has that divine ear?

If you want to survive an attack, you must start by believing that survival is possible. Although two percent is a very small number, it's significant. Too many people lose hope early on, when a few simple precautions can save their lives. The information presented in this section is compiled from the accounts of actual ninja attack survivors and advice from commando forces, including the Navy SEALs, the Green Berets and the Royal Marines, as well as a few suggestions from retired ninjas.

The following information is not designed to teach you how to defeat a ninja, only how to deter and survive an assault. Unless you're fully prepared and armed and have advanced combat training, do not attempt to engage the ninja directly. Prepare your home, prepare your body, and defend yourself the best you can. The following defensive principles, strategies and tactics offer the best chance of surviving a ninja attack.

PREPARING FOR THE ATTACK

If you suspect a ninja has been hired to take your life, do not panic. According to experts, ninja clans take an average of nine months to develop and plan their attack, allowing you plenty of time to prepare your house, your body and your mind for the assault.

The amount of time you can spend on preparations depends on your lifestyle, knowledge, ability and finances, but under no circumstances should your work be rushed. Prepare quickly but not sloppily. Every precaution should be taken thoroughly and completely. Double-check all your work. The tiniest mistake may cost you your life.

Unfortunately, you'll need to work alone. Although it'll be tempting to share with friends and family the fact that your life is in imminent danger, you must never let on that a ninja is after you. Ninjas rarely commit superfluous murders, but to keep ninjas out of the public spotlight, they'll murder anyone who learns of their existence. Furthermore, since ninjas are experts at disguise, your best friend or even your spouse may very well be one of them.

IDENTIFYING VULNERABLE AREAS

The ninja will often choose the location of the attack based on the target's lifestyle. If you can predict where the attack will happen, you stand a much better chance of thwarting your assailant. The ninja will follow you secretly for weeks or even months before picking the ideal location for the assault—preferably where you're alone and unprotected. If you live in a densely populated urban center like New York City, for example, and are always surrounded by witnesses, the attack will most likely occur in the privacy of your own home. If you live in a sparsely populated rural area, the location of the attack may be "open air" and less predictable. Examine your lifestyle—when are you at your most vulnerable?

NINJA-PROOFING YOUR HOUSE

Over 75 percent of all ninja attacks occur in the target's primary residence, so fortifying and protecting your home is vital. Ninja-proofing your domicile requires extreme diligence and thorough planning. If you leave a weakness, the ninja will exploit it. Examine every square foot of your property for defects and fix them. Although no house can ever be completely ninja-proof, taking every precaution will give you significant advantages over your assailant.

Securing the Perimeter

If a ninja cannot enter your property, he or she can't attack you in your home. A well-secured perimeter is the first step toward thwarting a home invasion. You must fortify the entire perimeter. If you only reinforce the front of your house, for example, the ninja will go around the back. Your perimeter fortification will depend on the size, shape and location of your property, as well as any local zoning laws and building codes that limit the height, design and materials of your desired modification.

Erections: Most ninja teams carry *kaginawa* (hemp climbing ropes) up to 30 feet long, so any erected barrier should be at least 40 feet high. The aesthetics of your erection will not matter—just make it big and intimidating.

Non-Electric Fences: Chain-link, wooden, picket and wrought-iron fences, no matter how high, are futile against a ninja. Ninjas are superior climbers and will simply scale the fence like a ladder. Reinforcing the top of a fence with barbed wire, pigeon wire or broken bottles will only slightly hinder a ninja's approach. Ninjas are naturally impervious to such hazards.

Electric Fences: The only fences known to hinder a ninja attack are electrified fences. Erected around your entire border, these high-voltage metal barriers may stop a home invasion. Make sure the fence is set to its highest voltage; if the shock is less than lethal, it'll simply annoy the ninja. But be aware that, with a little planning, ninjas can get past an electric fence by digging a hole underneath the fence or by simply wearing non-conducive clothing. (*Important Note:* Electric fences are at least as dangerous to you and your loved ones as they are to ninjas. If you have children or pets, an electric fence is a poor option.)

Walls: Because of the limitations of non-electric fences and the dangers of electric ones, well-constructed walls are the best option. Perimeter walls can be made from brick, stone, stucco, wood or concrete. A ninja can easily ascend brick and stone walls and break through stucco and wood with a forceful *shikan-ken* (extended knuckle punch) or any other host of strikes. A concrete wall at least 40 feet high is your best option for blocking a ninja attack.

Doors and Entry Gates: When erecting your ninja barriers, you'll need to include at least one entrance. The best type of door is made of reinforced metal. Your entrance should be protected by a thumb- or voice-activated personal identification system, or, better yet, a retina-scan biometric system, not just a key or combination lock system, which ninjas can easily pick.

Trees and Telephone Poles: A wall is futile against ninjas if there is a tree or telephone pole nearby. If possible, cut down all nearby trees and insist that the city install underground telephone cables without delay. Otherwise, you'll have to erect your barrier at least 20 feet from the nearest telephone pole or tree.

Moats: While moats, used in medieval castles and chateaux, may seem like an antiquated form of security, a properly constructed moat with a retractable bridge is the best fortification against ninjas. Make sure your moat is no less than 10 feet deep and 40 feet long. With their skill at digging, jumping and catapulting, ninjas have no trouble circumventing a moat with smaller dimensions.

Corrosive Moats: Since ninjas are expert swimmers and boaters, a moat filled with water is not particularly effective. Instead, fill your moat with any corrosive liquid. Strong acids and alkaline bases will corrode most substances and severely burn any human that touches them, including ninjas. (*Important Note:* Any substance that can injure a ninja can also injure you or you family. Take precautions to avoid accidental full-body exposure to moats.)

Animal-Filled Dry Moats: Buying a large quantity of any corrosive liquid may prove legally difficult or, at the very least, expensive. As an alternative, fill your moat with deadly animals such as unfed lions, tigers or gorillas to deter any ninja. The following animals make the best dry-moat fillers:

Cape Buffalo—This massive creature has a pair of dagger-sharp horns and an anger-management problem. A cape buffalo who believes the moat is his home will attack a ninja intruder.

Polar Bear—This gigantic beast is the most dangerous of all bears. An underfed polar bear will make bear food out of a foolish ninja. Obtaining a live polar bear can be difficult, though, as they're considered an endangered species.

African Lion (Male)—This aptly named "King of the Jungle/Savannah" is so powerful that he doesn't even bother hunting for himself. A few of these underfed jungle bad boys will make any moat nearly unsurpassable. The disadvantage is that neighbors may complain about nocturnal roaring.

Tiger—The tiger is even larger than the African lion and finds bathing enjoyable. Tigers are also an option if you plan to fill your moat with water.

Asian Cobra—This large, venomous reptile is among the deadliest of all snakes. Any sane ninja will think twice before crossing a moat full of cobras, just as anybody would.

Animal-Filled Wet Moats: The thoughtful ninja may be able to navigate an animal-filled dry moat by using animal tranquilizers or by simply bringing enough food to keep the beasts preoccupied. A murky wet moat filled with underwater killers may therefore be a better option. These four water dwellers can make minced meat (figuratively speaking) out of any ninja:

Poison Dart Frog—The back of this colorful creature secretes enough neurotoxins to kill ten ninjas. A moat filled end to end with poison dart frogs is similar to a corrosive moat.

Crocodile—If this primordial "mother of all reptiles" wants to make a ninja its dinner, it will.

Great White Shark—If the dimensions of your wet moat allow, keeping a few hungry great whites may be the best option.

Box Jellyfish—Every animal-filled saltwater moat should be supplemented with a few of these toxin-producing denizens of the deep.

Home Security Systems: While home security may not *prevent* a ninja attack, the advanced warning will give you vital seconds to make your final preparations. Consider the types of anti-ninja security that make sense for your budget and lifestyle.

Alarm Systems: Every home should be equipped with a modern, state-of-the-art alarm system that will alert the authorities when triggered. Your alarm system should work in conjunction with your perimeter security system. Mount motion detectors along your perimeter fortification and your garden, and install infrared and glass-break detectors throughout the house. Keep in mind, however, that most basic alarm systems can be disengaged easily with a few well-aimed

shuriken (ninja stars). In all modern ninja clans there's at least one agent who has been specially trained in alarm disengagement. Even the most advanced home security systems only pose a temporary hindrance, not a fail-safe method of protection.

Video Surveillance: Modern video surveillance systems are the best alarm security against a ninja attack. The live feed alerts the authorities, and video footage lets detectives gain insights into the ninja's identity. The ninja will not want to jeopardize his or her secrecy and the secrecy of the ninja fellowship.

Watchdogs: Dogs have been used as a defense against ninjas for centuries. Because of their keen sense of smell, watchdogs can alert their owner to the presence of an intruder. Most ninjas, however, can also sense the presence of a canine and take care to remain upwind. A large, loyal and vicious dog who is trained to attack can be your best ally in a battle against ninjas.

Larger Watch Animals: Lions and tigers are extremely intelligent creatures and can be trained as security pets. They also make valuable battle companions against even the deadliest of ninjas. Use great caution, though. Wild animals are not easily domesticated, and they may bite the hand that feeds them. The only thing worse than a lurking ninja in your house is a ninja and a rogue lion.

Window Barricades and Fire Escapes: Many apartment dwellers sever their fire escapes and barricade their windows, thinking these precautions will prevent the ninja from entering their unit. This precaution always backfires, though, by cutting off the victim's primary escape route.

Securing Your Home's Interior

Ninjas avoid combat situations if possible. Instead, they prefer to murder in stealth before their victim has a chance to react. To insure that their attack is a surprise, they often gain entry into your house or apartment when you're not home and conceal themselves to await your arrival. Destroy, recycle, fortify or at least become aware of common household features that are particularly vulnerable. The result will not be pretty, but it may save your life.

The Bedroom: For the ninja, the easiest victim is an unconscious one. That's why over 70 percent of home ninja attacks occur in the bedroom.

Bed Frames: The dark space under a bed frame offers the ninja a perfect hiding place in the heart of your bedroom. Once you retire for the evening, the ninja can merely wait for you to fall asleep before slaying you with his sword. Get rid of your bed frame! Donate it to your local homeless shelter.

Mattresses: The larger and puffier your mattress is, the more effectively it will conceal a ninja, who can slice open the mattress from the bottom, remove some stuffing, and crawl inside. By lying perfectly still, he or she is impossible to detect. The best plan is to recycle your mattress and sleep on the floor.

Sleeping Bags: Having removed your bed frame and your mattress, if you must sleep with bedding, thin sheets and blankets work best. Pygmy and midget ninjas can hide unsuspected in bulkier bedding, making quilts or down sleeping bags a bad choice. Be sure to flatten your sheets every morning. If you come home to ruffled or rearranged sheets, either someone has taken a nap ... or a ninja attack is imminent.

Closets: The closet is another common location for an attack. The ninja will most likely lurk in the darkened shadows cast by your clothing, waiting to spring out at you the minute you open the closet door. Seal up all closets. Move all your clothing to small drawers or other storage areas.

Bathtub or Shower: The bathtub or shower is a perfect place for the ninja to attack. Not only is it shadowed and concealed, but you'll most likely be naked and vulnerable when the attack comes. The best plan is to cease all use of showers and baths. Instead, do as the French do and cover your bodily odors with cologne, perfumes or deodorant. If you must bathe, do so only in a free-standing bathtub—no shower curtain!

Under the Desk or Table: The shadowy underside of opaque tables and desks make perfect hiding places for a ninja intruder. While it would be ideal to have a completely empty house, if you're unwilling to entirely purge your house of furniture, anything made from clear glass or transparent plastic can stay. Some victims insist on keeping family heirlooms and other antiques but then meet their demise because of foolish sentimentality.

Rafters and Beams: The ninja can take refuge above a crossbeam or rafter, waiting for the right moment to attack. If a rafter is not structurally necessary—check the blueprints—then get rid of it. Chop it down, saw it off, whatever it takes to dismantle it. If a beam or rafter is essential, take precautions to thwart ninja attackers. Some targets have super-glued nails to the topsides of exposed beams or placed pigeon wire there, making them uncomfortable hiding places.

Refrigerators/Dishwasher: Occasionally, ninjas surprise their victims by waiting inside a refrigerator or dishwasher. If possible, get rid of all bulky appliances. If you can't part with your refrigerator, at least exercise extreme caution when you open it. Hand-washing your dishes and using a small, minibar-size fridge is best.

Lights: Even though, as we all know, energy resources are scarce, keep lights on throughout your house at all times. Take special care to light the corners of rooms and the undersides of wooden furniture. Train yourself to sleep softly in a fully illuminated room. Even then, the ninja may cut your electrical wires, so carry a flashlight, candles and emergency flares on your person at all times.

Basements and Attics: Storage spaces filled with unused furniture, boxes and other junk can make it difficult to spot a hiding ninja. Empty these rooms, lock them tight and never look back. If you do have to enter the basement or attic, always carry a flashlight and a protective weapon. Avoid entering any basement or attic that is unfamiliar to you, especially if it's under the guise of "helping a friend move."

Telephones: While one ninja is attacking you, another will probably sever your landline connection. Carry a cell phone or satellite phone on your person at all times. If you sense a ninja attack, call the authorities immediately. Unfortunately, modern ninjas often carry high-power frequency jammers that can block your phone signal remotely from distances of up to 600 feet.

Household Weaponry

Common household items can be used as weapons or defensive protection in the event of a ninja attack. When preparing for a possible attack, survey each room of your house for makeshift weapons, but don't rely on these items alone. Carry handguns on your person at all times and keep an easily accessible shotgun nearby.

Staffs: Good for jabbing and smacking, as well as protection against a foe's staff. A well-chosen staff can help keep an enemy at a safe distance. A staff is useless against a ninja sword, though. Items that can be used as staffs include:

- Hockey stick
- Mop
- Hoe
- Broom
- Pool cue
- Rake

Bludgeons: When using a bludgeon, aim your blow at your assailant's skull, face or knee. Drive through the target zone; do not pull back upon contact. A well-chosen bludgeon can double as a staff. These items make effective bludgeons:

- Crowbar
- Shovel
- Hammer
- Baseball bat (strong metal bats can protect against swords, wooden bats only against staffs)
- Guitar or upright bass (noisy, though)
- Croquet mallet (may be too heavy and awkward to use against a ninja)

Blades: Blades make excellent weapons in short-range combat. Any powerfully driven stab will injure your assailant. Aim for the skull, neck, heart, stomach or another vital organ. If you brandish a bladed weapon, be prepared to use it: The ninja will draw a knife or sword as well. Use one of these:

- Axe or pickax
- Kitchen knife
- Hatchet
- Broken beer bottle

NINJA CHAINSAW MASSACRE

While the average urbanite will find using a chainsaw daunting, the loud, intimidating tool makes a superb anti-ninja weapon. Experts prefer two-stroke, gas-fed saws to the more finicky electric motors. Be sure to wear eye protection when attacking a ninja with a chainsaw; shards of ninja bone tend to be razor sharp.

Miscellaneous Makeshift Weaponry: The following household items may also come in handy:

- Tennis or racquetball racquet (A sports racquet makes a decent bludgeon, as long as you strike with the hard edge; racquet strings can be removed and used to choke your assailant from behind.)

- Billiard balls, baseballs, golf balls (Hurling these at your attacker's face or genital region can cause enough pain to allow your escape.)

- Aerosol sprays (When aimed at the face, hairspray, household cleaning products and insecticides can cause temporary blindness, allowing you a few extra seconds for escape. You may be tempted to follow the spray with a lit match or lighter, but this is unwise. Ninjas do not have a fear of fire, so the only damage you may inflict will be upon yourself.)

When evaluating household weaponry, be inventive. The preceding list is far from complete. If you don't have time to reach a better weapon, anything from a laptop to a coffee mug can cause significant damage when thrown forcefully and accurately.

NINJA-PROOFING YOUR BODY

To survive a ninja attack, you need to thoroughly ninja-proof your body. Too often a victim thoroughly prepares his or her home, only to leave his or her body exposed and vulnerable. Remember, ninjas *will* find a time and a place to attack. If they learn that you've turned your

residence into an impenetrable fortress, they'll find another location for the attack. Wear protective gear at all times, even in the privacy of your "ninja-proof" home.

Head and Neck Protection

Ninjas possess animalistic killing instincts. In both armed and unarmed combat, a ninja's first impulse is to strike at the jugular vein, the carotid artery, or the head/face. A kick or punch to the side of your head will leave you severely disoriented or trigger the "knock-out response," leaving you down for the count. A ninja will first target your neck, using his sword for a swift (and relatively painless) decapitation or a *shuriken* or arrows to puncture your jugular, carotid and/or trachea so you bleed/suffocate to death. Properly protecting your head and neck can keep you alive during such an attack.

Helmets: Many people use bicycle helmets or hard hats for ninja protection when moving through the city. But headgear that leaves your face exposed and only protects your head against blunt impact will not protect you against a well-trained foe. To protect your entire head, wear a full-face motorcycle, motocross or hockey helmet. These "fullies," as they're known among survivalist groups, protect your chin, the sides of your face and your ears. Helmets do severely limit peripheral vision, so keep your head on a swivel. They also interfere with socializing and office work, but most users adapt quickly to the visual distortion from the clear plastic visor. To avoid an unpleasant ninja conversation, if somebody asks you why you're wearing one, simply remove it, smile and exclaim, "Oops!"

Goggles: Ninjas carry *metsubushi* (blinding powders) and special explosives that will leave you in a dense fog of darkness and pain. By wearing protective eye goggles under your helmet, you stand a chance of protecting yourself from this age-old ninja tactic. Your eyewear should be made of a translucent, shatterproof material, like goggles designed for use with power tools or in chemical laboratories.

SURVIVING A COORDINATED ATTACK: COMPULSIVE ACTIONS

Following is an excerpt from a Project STEALTH survival analysis:

SUBJECT: Matthew D. McSurly

DOI: 9/13/2002

LOCATION: New York City

STEALTH ACTION LOG: Subject, Matthew Daniel McSurly, was handed over to us by NYPD after being flagged in our "likely target" database. It was determined that this incident was most certainly initiated by ninjas. The subject is a fit, 42-year-old white male residing in Manhattan. In his interview with STEALTH, the subject was visibly shaken and showing possible signs of PTSD. Aside from mental trauma, the subject shows no serious injuries. Subject has been previously diagnosed with hypochondria and severe obsessive-compulsive disorder. It appears that his disorders may have assisted in his remarkable survival.

Subject claims that he refused to enter his house after noticing a misplaced smudge mark on his doorknob, which alerted him to the possible presence of an intruder. Subject left his residence and moved to the street to find a police officer. After failing to find help, he began to run west. He then observed multiple masked individuals following him, with one moving along nearby rooftops. It is believed that no attack was initiated due to nearby bystanders. Subject continued west before turning into a narrow alley. He then took refuge in a pile of trash bags. Six hours later he was located by a garbage man who called for help.

ANALYSIS: Though the subject did not anticipate the attack, his extreme compulsion and paranoia allowed him to make quick judgments and enabled his survival. Furthermore, the safe zone he chose, a pile of trash bags, was an unexpected place to find a compulsively clean individual. By forcing himself outside of his comfort zone, the subject ensured his survival.

Protective Neckwear: Most sporting-good stores carry protective neckwear for motocross and dirt-bike enthusiasts. These braces prevent broken necks, but they won't stop a forceful sword or *shuriken* strike. Reinforce your neckwear with steel, Kevlar and ballistic nylon.

Torso and Organ Protection

As today's elite soldiers know, torso protection for your vital organs can be the difference between a live warrior and a dead one. Ninjas are trained to target soft, sensitive body parts. To deliver a clean, silent death blow, ninjas will most likely aim for your heart, known to most ninjas as the "human kill switch." If your heart is protected, ninjas will aim for another vital organ—lung, liver or bowels. Another classic ninja target is the testicle region, where a strike can cause excruciating pain, swelling and loss of fertility.

Bullet-Proof Vests: Wear a modern bulletproof vest under your everyday clothes at all times. Made of Kevlar, Dragon Skin or Zylon, this light, durable defensive armor will protect your torso against many types of ninja weaponry. Designed for policemen, bodyguards and other combat specialists, it is comfortable and hardly restricts mobility at all. Be aware that while Kevlar vests may stop projectiles, the material *can* be punctured by sharpened blades. Steel or ballistic clay should be used in combination.

Teflon Suits: The chemical compound known as Teflon, found in non-stick pans and many suitcases, is more durable than steel. If you're unable to purchase a bullet-proof vest, an improvised suit of duct tape and Teflon may suffice. Make sure your contraption covers your entire torso—chest, stomach, back and sides.

Cup: This ancient device protects man's most vulnerable organ. The kind of plastic cup used by athletes is not enough. Any steel blade will pierce the plastic like a knife through butter. Instead, reinforce your cup with puncture-proof materials.

NINJAS AND HUMAN BIOLOGY

The human body is soft, delicate and easily damaged. The ninja is very well-versed in human anatomy and will target any vulnerable area with remarkable accuracy. Take EVERY precaution you can to protect your body from injury.

THE NINJA HEARTTHROB

According to legend, male ninjas between the ages of 16 and 39 cannot kill female targets by stabbing them in the heart. It's believed that a female survivor's punctured heart will heal quickly, no matter how severe the initial wound. Two days after the stabbing, the only evidence of the attack is a slightly swollen heart and amorous feelings toward the attacker. In fact, the English phrase "heartthrob" derives from the Japanese phrase *shinzou ketsueki*, the technical term for the strange after-affects of such an attack.

THE VERMIFORM APPENDIX TROPHY

Although Western science believes the appendix to be a now-useless vestige of our primitive past, ninjas regard it as the single most important organ in the body because it enhances the "sixth sense." In fact, in some *ryu*, a ninja's standing is determined by the number of appendix trophies he has dangling from his porch.

Limb and Extremity Protection

Besides your vital organs, ninjas will try any way possible to cause you bodily harm. A well-powered *shikan-ken* (extended-knuckle punch) can crack most small- and medium-sized bones, and a stab to a major artery will kill you in minutes. The ninja will attack any exposed area. When choosing protective gear, cover every inch of your body—and more.

PROTECTING YOUR JUNK

Sexually transmitted diseases are embarrassing and worrisome at best and downright debilitating at worst. Wear a condom at all times, even during "walking around" times. You never know when a ninja will attack while treating your herpes.

Shin Guards: The ninja clan will often send a fledgling child ninja-in-training to attack a less-than-worthy adversary. If they decide you'll make an easy target, you'll find yourself assailed by these miniature ninjas, who deliver a barrage of powerful kicks to your shins. Wear shin guards at all times. It may save you the embarrassment of being felled by a foe half your size.

Knee, Wrist and Elbow Guards: Expect your attacker to trip you if you attempt to flee. Be on guard against well-placed, hard-to-spot *bengoshi* (clotheslines), well-aimed *shuriken* or simply marbles or banana peels thrown under your moving feet. To protect against painful bruises, scrapes, sprains or fractures to knees, wrists or elbows, wear reinforced, padded guards.

Anklewear: The ankle is one of the most vulnerable body parts. While fleeing your ninja pursuer, your running, jumping, turning and other evasive tactics can put your ankle under severe stress. A sprain or fracture will almost certainly mean your life. Always wear a tightly wrapped Ace bandage or a properly fitted brace around each ankle just in case.

Footwear: Appropriate footwear serves a dual purpose, protecting your feet against blows and weapons while also aiding in long-distance escape. Unless your feet are so callused they're tough as shoe leather, going shoeless leaves you vulnerable. Your ninja assailant can easily deter your escape by scattering *tetsubishi* (metal spikes) or *iga* balls along your path. Wear your footwear at all times, even when you bathe or sleep, as the attack will likely occur when you're most vulnerable.

Sandals, flip-flops or *strappy dress shoes*, however, are a bad choice. Not only do they make running hard, they also leave the tops of your feet dangerously exposed.

KEEPING YOUR FRIENDS, FAMILY AND CO-WORKERS IN THE DARK

You can expect that your preparations will seem strange to your friends, family and co-workers, arousing suspicion or concern. Coming up with a believable lie may save your loved one's life—and save you from being taken away in a straightjacket. One explanation is that you're climate-proofing your house or your body because of drastic climate changes caused by global warming. When asked about bizarre structural changes you're making to your home, say you're hurricane-proofing your house. When asked about the protective gear you're wearing, say you're protecting yourself against global warming–induced thunderstorms. Global warming may not always be a suitable excuse, especially if you know someone who doesn't believe in it and feels ideologically compelled to ridicule the notion. Tailor your fabrication to your audience, and take care to keep your story consistent in every detail.

Favored by ninjas because they're flexible and silent, *jika-tabi* may seem like the best option—but they're not. Ninjas have such intimate knowledge of this ancient footwear that they know both its benefits and pitfalls. They can strike the exposed toes with a bone-crushing heel jab or stab them with a bladed or pointed weapon. The main benefit of the *jiki-tabi* silence is lost on typically loud, clumsy Westerners.

With a name like "combat," you can trust that *combat boots* are ideal for protecting your feet. Statistically, it seems to be a proven fact. No victim of ninja violence has ever been found wearing combat boots.

A well-made pair of *running shoes* is a good anti-ninja footwear option because of its durability, light weight and arch support. Choose a pair with all-terrain grip, superior ankle support and orthopedic inserts. To ensure a quick escape, wear your running shoes at all times and make sure they're double-knotted.

TRAINING YOUR BODY AND YOUR MIND

Now that you've thoroughly protected your house and your body, it's time to start training for the attack. When it comes, you'll need every ounce of awareness, strength, quickness, stamina, endurance, mental toughness and all-around smarts you can muster to outlast your ninja opponent. Most people don't have it—and thus don't stand a chance. If you want to survive, discipline your body and mind. Physical and mental preparation for an attack is as important as any protective measure. Proper training requires extreme willpower and ceaseless hard work. Do not take your training lightly. You're not preparing for the Russian Ballet or the New England Patriots tryout camp. You're training for all-out war.

Simply being "in shape" will not suffice. You need to turn your body into a well-oiled machine, a machine that can run for dozens of miles at top speed, can survive for weeks on nothing but legumes and water, can take the batterings of a motorcycle test dummy, and can stay awake, alert and capable for days on end without a minute's repose. Reaching this state of physical perfection is no walk in the park, and will take weeks or months of exhausting, endless training and conditioning; but in the end you'll not only be able to say you fended off a ninja, but you'll have the enviable body of a Greek immortal.

FITNESS TRAINING

All the weaponry and defensive armor in the world is useless on a person who has no endurance and strength to fight back. Before you even think about picking up a rifle, pick up some weights and a pair of running shoes.

Speed: Your primary method of survival will be escape. The ninja may immobilize your escape vehicles, forcing you to flee on foot. Train by running in short bursts. Run five to ten miles each day, averaging five-minute miles. Run at least four times per week. On weekends, complete 20-mile runs, maintaining a pace of at least six minutes per mile. Never run along your prepared escape route for fear of revealing it to spies.

The ability to sprint all-out may just save your life. In addition to your five- to ten-mile daily runs, do daily sprint training: perform five 100-yard dashes in less than 10.5 seconds each, five 400-meter runs in less than 55 seconds each and five 800-meter runs in less than two minutes each. A good sprint can bring you quickly to a nearby "bug-out," or "safe zone" (see Chapter 5). Practice running in unpredictable zigzags since, when the attack comes, your pursuer will probably be throwing *shuriken* or firing arrows at your body.

It's also a good idea to take a few long bicycle rides every week, just in case you need to escape using pedal power.

Agility: The importance of being quick cannot be overstated. In close-range combat, your skill at dodging a weapon, punch or kick will spell the difference between life and death. All manner of sports, including basketball, racquetball, soccer, hockey and even polo, will help develop foot speed as well as hand-eye coordination.

Flexibility: Being limber may help you dodge a ninja sword thrust and can prevent a sprain or pulled muscle during a strenuous battle. A thorough stretch every morning and evening will keep you flexible. You may want to take up yoga if you're a yuppie, hippie, hipster or girl.

Strength: Do not use your ninja-training regimen as an excuse to become that muscle-bound, no-neck, meat-headed dunderbrain you may have always wanted to be. The goal of your strength-training routine is to improve your anaerobic endurance, not to become a bodybuilder or power lifter. Any extra, unnecessary bulk can cost you your life. Weight training is not necessary. Push-ups, sits-ups, pull-ups, dips, squats, lunges and leg lifts will do the job. Your goal should be speed and repetitions. Not surprisingly, a "supposed ninja" holds the world record for consecutive push-ups—10,507 of them! You should be able to do at least half as many.

THE FAMOUS "NINJA BATTLE" DIET

You'll need an extreme dietary makeover to supplement your fitness regimen. It may require the most self-discipline of any of the lifestyle changes described in this chapter. Ignore the deep grumbles in your belly that command you to indulge in a smoky bacon cheddar cheeseburger. Make your meals light, healthy and, above all, flavorless. Difficult though this diet may be, given your rigorous fitness routine, purging yourself of all indulgences is the only way to reach your peak performance level.

Caloric Intake and Protein: By engaging in a proper anti-ninja training routine, you'll burn between 3,000 and 5,000 calories daily. Your main nutritional concern will be getting enough calories while keeping your fat intake to a minimum. Look for foods that are high in protein, yet low in fat. Any foods with trans fat are entirely off limits. Base your diet on staples such as whole-grain breads and pasta, potatoes, boiled vegetables and cereals. Your protein intake should be limited to eggs, carnivorous fish and grilled lean red meats such as bison.

Eating Naturally: Steer away from any prepackaged, processed foods. They often contain dangerously high levels of sodium and chemical additives that cause lethargy and arterial buildup. Chemical additives and toxins are often secreted during perspiration, leaving a distinctive smell that a ninja can easily detect. If packaged food has more than four ingredients, or any ingredient you can't pronounce, steer clear.

Meal Quantity and Distribution: The Western three-meals-a-day routine is a major pitfall when it comes to physical training because it makes for significant energy peaks and troughs. Instead, eat seven to nine small meals evenly spaced throughout the day and snack constantly to keep your energy levels up.

Snacking: The Ninja Battle Diet is one of the few around that actually encourage snacking. Fruits, vegetables, nuts, legumes, hard-boiled eggs and certain chocolates will keep you performing at your highest level throughout the day. Carry a few bags of high-calorie trail mix at all times. They may come in handy during a long chase or impromptu bug-out.

Calcium: The ninja, well versed in *koppojutsu* (the art of breaking bones), will target weak or brittle bones. Upping your calcium intake can mean the difference between a bad "Indian burn" and a broken wrist. Drink a gallon of milk daily. Sunbathe at least 25 minutes a day to get enough vitamin D to promote calcium absorption.

Breaking Your Diet: Stay strong. Do not break your diet. Ever.

ALCOHOL AND DRUGS

While studies have shown that alcohol, consumed in moderation, has some beneficial effects, the same does not hold true in a ninja attack. The perceived confidence and bravery you get from social alcohol drinking will not help you in a life-threatening attack.

On the other hand, studies show that small doses of stimulants such as caffeine, nicotine, cocaine and amphetamines can come in handy when faced with a ninja attacker. Stimulants increase mental awareness, alertness, motivation, heart rate, blood pressure and pain tolerance, making you a worthier opponent and, at the same time, decreasing appetite and the need for sleep during a prolonged chase or escape. Only ingest the stimulant during the actual attack. You must be completely drug-free during the duration of your training. Ninjas do not drink or take mind-altering drugs. Neither should you. Just say no.

COMBAT TRAINING

If you find yourself head to head with a ninja assailant, you'll need to be proficient in various combat arts. Ninjas are trained in various striking, grappling and weaponry techniques, so you must also practice all three. When choosing an art and an instructor, keep in mind that you're training for mortal combat. Schools, and instructors that emphasize the "sparring," "gaming" or "playing" aspect of a fighting art should be only a last resort. Many people take up *ninjutsu* to "fight fire with fire." As you'll never reach ninja levels of skill, training in *ninjutsu* is a bad choice. Instead, you'll need to learn a variety of martial arts that work well as counters to ninjutsu. When fighting a ninja, defense is always the best offense.

SIMULATED BATTLES

Remember, you're training for a life-threatening battle. You must develop the ability to fight through injuries and pain. Most martial arts instructors prefer to train students in relatively pain-free simulations. Even Krav Maga trainees wear padding on the strike points. But you must learn to fight under agonizing amounts of pain. To perform well under the stress of an actual ninja assault, you must train in non-lethal "real-life" battles with your instructor, friends or strangers. Be careful not to go to jail, though. Time incarcerated means training time lost.

Grappling: Grappling is quite effective in up-close, unarmed combat. The ability to initiate a take-down or pin from a variety of positions is vital. Various arm and joint lock techniques can also be effective for either immobilizing an opponent or snapping his joints, ligaments and thinner bones. The best way to study the grappling arts is to supplement jujitsu with aikido. Jujitsu teaches joint locks, chokes and submission holds, and also includes striking methods; aikido teaches how to use your opponent's strength and momentum to your advantage so that you expend minimal energy during battle. Important: Neither Greco-Roman nor WWF-style wrestling will suffice (unless you suspect that your attacker will be dazzled by tight, bright spandex).

Striking: Knowledge of various striking methods not only enables you to injure your assailant but also gives you an understanding of how he or she will strike, giving you a better chance to evade, hinder or otherwise diminish the strength of the strikes. Muay Thai, or Thai boxing, is the most effective martial art for striking. While Western boxing uses two striking points (the fists) and other striking arts employ four striking points (fists and feet), Muay Thai employs a staggering *nine* striking points, including the fists, feet/shins, knees, elbows and head. Note that head-butting is currently banned in professional Muay Thai fighting and scarcely taught to new students. Be sure to let your instructor know you wish to add it into your training and slip him a little extra cash.

Krav Maga: Invented in Israel and used by the Israel Defense Forces (IDF), the FBI, American and British Special Forces, and a variety of bad-ass special operatives, Krav Maga emphasizes self-defense and escape in real-life, you-or-me, live-or-die situations. Because Krav Maga evolved under the watchful, paranoid eye of the IDF, it's very much designed to avoid death. The rigorous training includes painful scenarios. You may be force-fed debilitating amounts of alcohol to disorient your senses, have one arm tied behind your back, and then be pitted against multiple armed and deadly opponents.

BLINDFOLDED TRAINING

Modern humans depend heavily on vision for getting around and functioning. To ensure survival, you must improve your other senses as well. To do so, perform your daily training routine blindfolded one full day each week. Do all your daily activities with the same vigor as you would if you still had your vision. Complete lengthy trail runs, weight training and martial arts matches with a tightly wrapped blindfold, trusting your other senses to help you survive. After some time, you'll learn to navigate your world entirely vision-free.

MENTAL TRAINING

Training your mind is the single most important part of anti-ninja preparation. Above all else, ninjas are mentally superior warriors. The physical aspects of a ninja's regimen account for only one third of his or her training. Another third involves controlling his or her opponent's mind through various psychological techniques, and the final third is related to manipulating the universe. It's unlikely that you, as an untrained target, will be attacked by a Phase III ninja, capable of controlling the universe. These ninjas are reserved for only the deadliest of adversaries. You'll most likely be attacked by a Phase II ninja. While Phase II ninjas cannot yet tamper with the universe, they do possess high mind powers to fool you, befriend you or otherwise manipulate you. Advanced Phase

II operatives can control your mind. To survive an attack by a Phase II ninja, you must learn to defend yourself against psychological warfare. Besides learning ways to anticipate and recognize psychological warfare, you'll have to develop your own sensory perceptions and awareness.

Awareness, Attention and Intent: To anticipate a ninja attack, you must boost your awareness and alertness levels. An attack can come at any time, anywhere, from anyone. Learn to recognize signs of an impending attack and spring into action the second it begins.

Sight: Train your eyes to be like an eagle's by day and an owl's by night. If you have less-than-perfect vision, laser surgery is a must. Do not rely on glasses, contacts, monocles, night-vision goggles, binoculars or telescopes, as you may not be able to reach them during an attack. There are numerous methods for improving your vision. For instance, eat plenty of carrots. And above all, don't masturbate.

Sound: Sound may be your only cue during a battle. Familiarize yourself with the various sounds of the ninja arsenal. You should be able to pinpoint the release location and trajectory of every ninja weapon.

Touch: Improving your sense of touch means more than knowing when you've come into contact with another object. Train yourself to sense sudden environmental phenomena like airflow shifts and pressure changes. In a darkened room the ninja can sense an opponent's movements simply by observing airflow patterns. Can you?

Smell: Ninjas use their sense of smell to detect food and water as well as watchdogs, rotting wood and other potential threats. Train yourself to inhale through your nose, letting the air rest in your nostrils for a moment. If you're in an unfamiliar, dark environment, this breathing technique will help you sense a variety of obstacles.

Taste: Although your taste buds will be overpowered by adrenaline and rendered useless during an attack, a ninja may attempt to poison you when you're not expecting it. Use your sense of taste to detect poison or drugs, which may be strangely bitter, sour or delicious.

CHAPTER 5

BUGGING OUT—
MAKING YOUR ESCAPE

Too much protection is never enough. Always be ready to run.
　　—*Mac Braz, BrazCorp Security Services, private international military company*

✳ ✳ ✳

You've fended off the initial ninja assault and bought precious moments to make your escape. Now seize the opportunity to get out of Dodge. Even if you were Jackie Chan, Mike Tyson or Hulk Hogan, your ninja opponent would outsmart, outmaneuver and overpower you if you stuck around.

PLANNING THE ROUTE

Expect pursuing ninjas to come after you on foot or horseback. Having a faster mode of transportation is your only chance to make your getaway. Once you've reached your vehicle (beware of the ninja standing guard nearby), your escape should be so well rehearsed that it's second nature. Your route should avoid any street that could be backed up with traffic. Idling at red lights or stop signs is never an option. Plan your route down streets with little cross traffic where lights and signs are "stoptional." Travel under an alias and scrub your person of identification. Your end destination should be either a rural location or an urban area at least 200 miles away. Do not make phone calls. Even if you dispose of your cell phone and credit cards, though, the ninja team will track you by scent and sign with almost certain success, so keep on the move and stay aware.

CHOOSING YOUR BUG-OUT ZONE

A "bug-out" or "safe" zone is any place a ninja is unlikely to attack for at least 72 hours, giving you time to rest and plan. The best bug-out zones are places that are populated at all hours, such as Times Square, the Vegas Strip or a 24-hour diner. Rural areas are another option. Your destination should be either a heavily fortified safe house that is off the grid or a remote wilderness setting where you can find shelter and sustenance. See "Wilderness Evasion," page 91.

LEAVING YOUR HOME OR BUSINESS

Ninjas rarely attack alone. A group, or "clan," usually provides backup support (see page 25). While the assailant assigned to assassinate you is infiltrating your house, between one and twenty other agents will be stationed nearby, securing the perimeter.

If your car is parked in your garage or driveway, one or more agents will likely be blocking access to it. Plan a less obvious escape to an offsite vehicle. Fleeing in a golf-cart or lawnmower may seem ridiculous, but it's a wiser option than trying to reach the car parked in your driveway.

Underground Tunnel: If you have enough time to build a sturdy subterranean passageway, do so. Make sure it leads at least 100 yards away from your house. To ensure your ninja assailant cannot follow you, the entrance should be rigged to collapse after your escape.

Disguise: As soon as you make your escape, plan to change your appearance as much as possible. Ninjas are specially trained to recognize facial structure, eyes, stature and gait. Men should grow or shave facial hair. Change your hair style and color (keep dyes and scissors on hand at all times), apply copious amounts of tanning lotion, get new glasses (or, if you don't need glasses, a false pair) that cover up as much of your face as possible. To conceal your stature, buy baggy clothing and develop a slouch and a slight limp. If possible, change your apparent gender.

Bug-Out Bag: Available online and at countless survivalist outlets, these handy backpacks contain everything you need to survive (food, water-purification tablets, first-aid kits, blankets and the like) to leave your house suddenly and head into the unknown. Buy at least two of these packs, keeping one in your designated escape vehicle and one at home.

TRANSPORTATION

Bugging out on foot is daunting, dangerous and painfully slow. Procuring and maintaining a trustworthy mode of transportation should be at the top of your priorities' list.

AUTOMOBILES

Unless you have access to an army tank or helicopter, the sturdiest, safest escape vehicle for eluding a pursuing ninja or ninja squad is your automobile. Keep it in excellent running order, fully fueled and parked in a wide parking space to ensure a rapid exit. Never parallel park your car in a place where pulling out would mean making a multi-point turn.

Install top-of-the-line run-flat tires. A pursuing ninja will target the soft, vulnerable wheels with arrows, throwing stars or puncture jacks. A car alarm system is a must, though ninjas have been known to successfully breach that defense. Be sure to keep spare gasoline in a secure location in your trunk. It can be used to refuel the vehicle or as a diversionary weapon. Tinted windows are a costly mistake. A ninja can pick out your vehicle anywhere, so hiding your face behind darkened glass is useless. It only gives police reason to pull you over during an escape and also provides ample cover for a back-seat assassin.

Sedans/Sports Cars: Until America's flailing auto companies begin producing more reliable vehicles, a midrange, foreign-made sedan is recommended. An early peek at the 2010 Sandoval Car & Truck Defensive Ratings show the Hyundai Genesis Coupe to be the best "defensive car"

based on fuel efficiency, speed, price and weapon-storage capacity. With better gas mileage and packing more relative power than SUVs, light trucks or station wagons, sedans make ideal escape vehicles.

MANUAL OR AUTOMATIC?

The choice is yours. Many people fleeing ninja attacks are in a state of panic or near-shock, unable to cope with extra tasks such as gear shifting. On the flip side, others find a stick shift's added control over speed and traction much better for evasion.

Hatchbacks/Station Wagons: Reliable and roomy, the standard hatchback or station wagon comes with some major benefits and one huge drawback—an open trunk. While the trunk allows for easy weapons storage and access, it also provides an ideal hiding place for an assassin. If you drive one of these vehicles, check the back seats and storage space carefully and frequently. Installing a wire mesh in the rear windows may prevent an attacking ninja from invading your vehicle during your escape.

SUVs, Trucks and Off-Road Vehicles: If your primary escape route takes you out of the city and onto rural, rough roads, a heavy-duty vehicle is a must. The added suspension and rigid frame will help you outmaneuver a ninja. The primary disadvantages come from the disappointing gas mileage and awkward size for driving through the city. Stopping for gas makes you more vulnerable to attack, so avoid pit stops at all costs. As with other vehicles, carrying extra gasoline is essential, but with a big SUV you need to carry lots more of it.

MOTORCYCLES

An agile, two-wheeled speed demon is perfect for making an emergency escape through crowded city streets. If the ninja who assailed you has a backup team supporting him, chances are they're covering your escape routes, ready to attack. If you plan to use a motorcycle as your escape vehicle, practice making strong emergency swerves to avoid descending assassins. You'll also need thick gear and body armor that can fend off projectiles. Ride low and fast and choose a sport bike over a cruiser or touring bike. Be on special guard against *bengoshi*, undetectable "clotheslines" a ninja may string up along your path. Other dangers include spiked *tetsubishi* or *iga* balls set out in the road to puncture tires.

BOATS

Don't assume you can escape a ninja attack simply by taking refuge in the water. In 1976, three members of the Coniglio crime family did exactly that. They tried to escape a pair of ninja assassins by crossing by speedboat from Catania, Sicily, to Sant'Elia, Reggio Calabria. Halfway across, they stopped to rest. Three days later, their abandoned boat drifted into rocks in the northern Straits of Messina and broke apart. No bodies were ever recovered.

Water training, or *mizu-ren*, is an integral part of every ninja's regimen, and to become a ninja one must pass extremely challenging water tests, swimming for both speed and endurance in waters both still and rough, fresh and salt. They must learn to hold their breath for at least four minutes, to operate various watercraft, including kayaks, canoes, sailboats, motorboats, steamers, yachts, schooners, windjammers and even barges, and to navigate the ocean by day and night, with or without a compass. If you attempt an escape by sea, follow these rules:

* **Keep moving.** Ninjas can achieve speeds of up to 10 knots while swimming. A ninja pursuing you in a hand-powered watercraft can outpace even the most powerful U.S. Coast Guard go-fast boats, let alone your private vessel.

* **Avoid using motorized boats.** "Going stealth" (using a nonmotorized boat) lets you fight silence with silence. The sound of a running motor can be heard for miles underwater, and ninjas are trained to distinguish the sound while fully immersed. Travel by sail whenever possible. A wide zigzag sailing pattern may help in successful evasion.

* **Send nothing overboard.** Jetsam—anything jettisoned from a boat in mid-voyage—is a dead giveaway to your course. Assume the ninjas pursuing you have studied tide tables and current charts for the area. Any debris they find can put them on your trail.

PLANES

Statistically, the plane is the most effective mode of long-term escape. Carrying you hundreds or thousand miles away from the threat, the plane also gives you precious time to rest and plan before your arrival. The primary threats come from the potential delay in takeoff and the possibility that the ninja has made it onto the plane with you. If you're traveling on a commercial jetliner, do not drink, eat or use the restroom; remain in your seat, visible to the other passengers. If your plane is chartered, be sure to wear a parachute and inform your pilot of the danger. A ninja attack at 30,000 feet is almost always fatal, so be ready to bail out if necessary.

AIR ACCIDENTS

Ninja attacks are responsible for nearly one-third of all private plane "disappearances," compared to a relatively low percentage of automobile fatalities. Commercial jetliners are now required to have onboard defibrillators in response to the rash of ninja-induced, in-flight heart attacks during the 1980s.

TRAINS OR METRO

If you live in a major metropolitan area such as New York City, London or Tokyo, you may have to rely entirely on rail travel for your escape. While by no means ideal, you can use a commuter train or subway to your advantage.

- Memorize timetables down to the minute for at least ten different trains. When you go to a station to board a train, you should not have to wait on the platform for more than 30 seconds.
- Do not use your normal commuting station. Make an escape on foot or bicycle to another location and board there.
- Do not board a train traveling a line you ride frequently. If your daily route takes you from Brooklyn to Manhattan, choose a train bound for Jamaica or Queens.
- Make eye contact with as many fellow travelers as possible. You want to be noticed to deter any ninja that has followed you onboard.
- If you're traveling in an empty car, use a newspaper, book or hood to shield your face.
- Remain vigilant.

BICYCLES

With its durable light frame, agile handling and no need for fuel, a bicycle is highly recommended as a backup escape vehicle. If you live in a valley or hilly area, a bicycle getaway is less than ideal because of the slow, trudging ascents. Practice riding your escape route at least once a week to become aware of obstacles, develop short cuts and build the physical endurance you'll need when the time comes. Tires made with lightweight steel liners to avoid punctures and flats are essential. If your route takes you into wooded or uneven terrain, use a mountain bike. A fast, multi-speed road bike is ideal for urban flight. When you arrive at your bug-out destination, do not lock your bike outside or it will be identified.

ROLLERBLADES, SKATEBOARDS OR SCOOTERS

Any vehicle that will only increase your forward velocity by a few miles per hour is not very helpful in a crisis escape. The chances of falling or being caught or delayed are far greater than when escaping on foot. Leave the wheels behind and get a good pair of running shoes instead.

JETPACKS

If you have the funding and flying experience, a jetpack can make for a nearly foolproof aerial escape. The drawbacks to the pack are that the takeoff is loud, the condensation trail is easy to spot, and maintenance is costly. Always have a destination in mind and wear a helmet.

HORSES

Unlike ninjas, most Americans do not own or even know how to ride horses. Forget about them unless you're thoroughly proficient at horseback riding. Remember, one or more ninjas will probably be pursuing on horseback, so make sure your steed is in good shape and well fed and rested. Do not attempt to confront an attacking ninja on horseback. Simply dismount and proceed on foot. Keep in mind that a horse is always conspicuous in a major metropolitan area.

ON FOOT

Personal locomotion may not be the fastest mode of escape, but it's the most reliable. If you're making your escape on foot, you may also be suffering from injuries inflicted during the initial ninja assault. Apply pressure bandages before you begin a lengthy escape. Blood loss is the leading cause of fatigue in a getaway on foot.

Do not practice running your escape route in advance. The ninja team will follow and become familiar with your route. Instead, plan your route out thoroughly, acquainting yourself with streets and landmarks from your car and by studying maps. You should be able to run at a steady pace for at least 15 miles—approximately 1.5 hours—without tiring. Wear comfortable, supportive shoes—avoiding shin splints and foot cramps can mean the difference between life and death.

WILDERNESS EVASION

Escaping into the wild has both its major benefits and crippling drawbacks. If you choose to make your way into the wilderness, keep a few things in mind: No matter how much "survivalism" you fancy yourself to know, the ninja is better versed. While you may pine for modern luxuries such as fire and shelter, the ninja requires neither. Tracking a ninja is impossible. Tracking a scared human, on the run, with little gear or experience, is like tracking an elephant in a petting zoo.

WATER AND FOOD

When it comes to surviving off the land, water will be your first and foremost concern. Unfortunately, the ninja knows that. If you've bugged-out properly, you've taken enough water-tight containers to collect enough H_2O for an *entire* day. Because the ninja will be looking out for sources of water as potential staging areas for ambushes, it's important to locate a source, collect your water quickly and move on. Do not return to a water source that you've already used; it's now being guarded or has been poisoned.

You'll also need to find enough food to nourish your body while it's on the run. Look for sources that are high in protein, such as wild game, fish or insects. Do not spend too much time hunting larger animals; while you're scouting for a deer's tracks, the ninja is looking for yours. In addition, a large carcass can be more cumbersome than it is beneficial. Take what you need and discard the rest; remember that time taken to cook your catch is valuable time spent not escaping.

Edible plant life is one of the best ways of sustaining yourself while in the wild. A local botany book is one of the most valuable tools you can keep with your person. Be wary, though; prepared ninjas may plant poisonous imitation flora if they detect you in the area.

FIRE

Because smoke is always a dead-giveaway to the classically trained ninja, never build a fire that is larger than the size of two fists. Always use dry brush and kindling; wet or green plants will increase the quantity of smoke that will be visible. If weather is favorable, always extinguish your fire before you head to your shelter to sleep or rest. Bury any remains of your campfires to impede the ninja's tracking.

If you've successfully killed a wild animal and need to cook the meat, it's vital that you do not pause during daylight walking hours to prepare it. If you can wait until nightfall, do so, wrapping the meat in a cloth to prevent insects from getting at it. If you must cook the meat on the move, you'll need to build a "traveling stove."

NINJA-PROOF SHELTERS

Your most vulnerable time in the wild is when you're asleep or resting. Your ninja assassins rarely rest, giving them precious hours to close in on you. In addition, while the ninja may not attack you while you're asleep, being assaulted as you're just waking up is extremely unpleasant. Building a safe, concealing shelter is the key to getting a good night's rest and surviving to see another day.

UNDERGROUND BURROWS

In warm, dry climates, underground burrows make the best possible shelters. Dig a trench two to three feet deep, four feet wide and six to seven feet in length. At ground level, build a roof using a tarp, cloth or lattice of branches and twigs. The shelter should be masked with fallen leaves and ground debris to match the surroundings. Cover the entranceway with brambles or a small bush.

TREETOP SHELTERS

Ninjas don't rely on the treetops without reason. Above the sightline, and tucked away in the dense canopy, treetop shelters provide ample cover and a superior vantage point. Sounds and smells are dampened and dispersed. Fell as many long, sturdy branches as possible to build a platform across level boughs. Be sure to cover your raised shelter with enough foliage to hide your body and give the impression of a giant bird's nest. Take special care not to fall out of your perch; a broken bone is a serious problem miles into the wilderness, especially when being pursued by ninjas.

CAVES

Rock caverns shield you from the elements, wildlife and ninjas very effectively. If you can find a spacious cave that is deep enough to fully conceal your location, take advantage of the amazing find. Before entering, check for tracks and signs of carnivorous animals that may be using the cave for their own den. In addition, check for any ninjas that may be sharing the cave; nothing is more embarrassing than walking in on a dressing ninja and then having them kill you.

IN THE OPEN

While survival guides encourage making windbreaks, raised beds and covered shelters, you should avoid any unnecessary construction projects while on the run. If making a concealed shelter is out of the question, find a pile of leaves, lie on the ground and cover up—it's the best way to get a night's rest without the risk of being spotted.

UNDER WATER

Few people are comfortable with camping out beneath the waves. But if you have enough SCUBA experience, extra tanks and no fear of getting the bends, a thick kelp forest or murky lake bottom can make for an excellent, short-term, bug-out location.

CHAPTER 6

GOING ON THE OFFENSE: MODERN TACTICS AND THE NINJA

My rifle is my best friend. It is my life.
—*From My Rifle, creed of the United States Marine Corp.*

✳ ✳ ✳

Now that you've fended off the first devastating attack, the ninja's primary weapon—the element of surprise—is diminished. You've gained precious seconds and distance from your enemy, but making a complete escape may not be an option. Your survival now depends on your ability to mount a strong counteroffensive. This is not the moment to become a Spartan warrior, fighting sword with sword, stick with stick. Victory can only be won by grabbing the heavy machinery.

MODERN WEAPONRY

While unlikely, it is *possible* to kill a ninja without advanced training. The key is weaponry—when you get done preparing, your house should be as heavily stocked as Charlton Heston's coffin.

GUNS
Shotgun

Ninjas are trained to knock down high-velocity *shuriken* with their bare hands and deflect arrows with a knife blade. Some can even dodge a single well-aimed bullet. A shotgun is the perfect counter to the ninja's agility at close range. It delivers a wide pellet spray, so the assassin must move up to four feet in a split second to avoid it. Shotgun blasts are debilitating but not always fatal to a physically fit ninja. Even if you disable an arm, leg or eye, expect a continued fight. Reload as quickly as you can.

EASE OF USE	EFFECTIVENESS	LETHALITY	OVERALL ANTI-NINJA RATING
9	8	6	23/30 (ESSENTIAL)

Rifle: Semi-Automatic, Automatic or Light Machine Gun

The staple weapon of the U.S. Army infantry and well-proven in combat, an assault rifle is a must-have for your anti-ninja arsenal. Assault rifles are stable and accurate, and their rapid fire rate and large magazine make them effective against the wily ninja. When firing an automatic burst, first aim and fire straight at the ninja, then move the rifle barrel in a figure eight, covering both the high and low escape routes on each side of him. Keep extra ammunition magazines handy at all times.

EASE OF USE	EFFECTIVENESS	LETHALITY	OVERALL ANTI-NINJA RATING
8	9	9	26/30 (ESSENTIAL)

ANTICIPATE YOUR SHOT

Ninjas under fire will take evasive action with stunning, natural ease. Anticipating their next move will be crucial to a successful counterattack.

1. Expect them to block your first shot by hand or dodge it.
2. As ninja training and muscle memory kick in, they will:
   a. Perform a *kaiten,* or evasive roll, toward their escape route—or toward you, if you're within range;
   b. Leap onto a raised stationary object, rafter or ceiling beam;
   c. Deploy a smoke bomb or blinding powder; or
   d. Counter with *shuriken* or arrows.
3. Quickly fire a figure-eight burst from your weapon to cover their escape routes.
4. If they have ignited a smoke bomb, take evasive action. If you can't see ninjas, there's a remote chance that they can't see you either.

Rifle: Hunting and Sniper

Hunting and sniper rifles are deadly, but you need distance and surprise to use them most effectively. Hunting a professional assassin is a futile endeavor, and unless you're trained in military marksmanship, chances are you'll be outwitted and outmaneuvered. In the rare case that you do get an unsuspecting ninja in your sights, aim for the body. Fire and maneuver. Even a seriously wounded ninja can pinpoint the source of a shot by sound.

EASE OF USE	EFFECTIVENESS	LETHALITY	OVERALL ANTI-NINJA RATING
5	7	9	21/30 (OPTIONAL)

Handgun: Revolver

Quick to draw and easy to shoot, a revolver may seem like an excellent option. But a slow rate of fire and limited ammunition capacity makes the revolver a last-resort option. In optimal circumstances, you can expect that it will take 10 to 12 quick shots to hit an attacking ninja who is less than ten feet away. Add five bullets for every additional meter away. Six shots will not be enough.

EASE OF USE	EFFECTIVENESS	LETHALITY	OVERALL ANTI-NINJA RATING
7	3	5	15/30 (NOT RECOMMENDED)

Handgun: Semi-Automatic Pistol

Small, easily concealed and reliable, handguns such as the Glock, Mauser or Beretta should always be carried close at hand (with a permit, of course) in case of a ninja assault. The rapid rate of fire and large magazine capacity make these guns the best final line of defense against an attacking ninja. Keep extra magazines fully loaded and accessible, preferably in pouches that can be attached to the body quickly. If your weapon can fire multiple-round bursts, use the "full automatic" setting. Always aim for the body; a confirmed ninja head shot has never been recorded.[1]

EASE OF USE	EFFECTIVENESS	LETHALITY	OVERALL ANTI-NINJA RATING
9	7	8	24/30 (ESSENTIAL)

GRENADES AND ANTI-PERSONNEL EXPLOSIVES
Hand-Lobbed Grenades

If you try to use grenades or explosives against a ninja, you place yourself in a dangerous fire-on-fire situation. The ninja is well versed in the art of martial pyrotechnics, so fighting back with anti-personnel explosives can be very tricky. The grenade's delayed trigger allows the ninja ample time to escape or, worse yet, counterdeploy the live

---

[1] In April 1969, during the Vietnam Conflict, Sgt. Darrell Hutchkins, a Marine sniper, reported an unconfirmed head shot on a treetop-traveling "ninja" from a range of only 300 meters. In his official report, he wrote that he spotted a direct hit and pink spray through his scope but was unable to locate a body directly after contact. Many historians consider the "pink spray" to have been, simply, a ninja diversion, or that the man was not a ninja to begin with. To this day, it is the only suspected ninja head shot in recorded history.

ordinance (that is, hurl the grenade back at you). Unless you're extremely proficient at using hand-held explosives, don't. If you must stockpile them, steer clear of fragmentation or concussion grenades and use only nonlethal stun or sting grenades. Their disorienting effect can give you time to escape. Nonlethal grenades have limited effect on ninjas hiding in high places, though.

EASE OF USE	EFFECTIVENESS	LETHALITY	OVERALL ANTI-NINJA RATING
6	6	6	18/30 (OPTIONAL)

Rocket-Propelled Grenades and Grenade Launchers

Tube-fired anti-tank weapons are more effective at countering a ninja than hand-lobbed grenades because of the high projectile velocity, accuracy and range. But they're bulky and difficult to use quickly and safely. Although the weapons' original purpose as "tank busters" makes them unsuitable for use in close spaces, outdoors in a rural environment they can target a ninja, either hidden or in the open, within a range of up to 500 meters. With a velocity of 300 meters/second, a projectile can take a nearby ninja by surprise despite the noise and flash of the launch. After firing, maneuver to a new position immediately. Do not attempt to reload the weapon; discard it at once.

EASE OF USE	EFFECTIVENESS	LETHALITY	OVERALL ANTI-NINJA RATING
5	7	8	20/30 (OPTIONAL)

Mines

Never deploy mines to combat a ninja attack. Anti-personnel mines are most effective when placed on the ground, in the case of the Claymore, or buried in the earth, like the M16A1. Both weapons are only triggered when the assailant enters the mined area on foot—which you can't count on a ninja to do. Fleet-footed and extremely observant, ninjas can spot hidden land mines 85 percent of the time. And a ninja will only attack on the ground 30 percent of the time. If you plant land mines in your garden, you stand a better chance of blowing off your own leg as you get the morning paper than of successfully intercepting a ninja.

EASE OF USE	EFFECTIVENESS	LETHALITY	OVERALL ANTI-NINJA RATING
5	2	4	11/30 (NOT RECOMMENDED)

FIRE
Flame Throwers and Molotov Cocktails

If you're prepared to sacrifice your home, office or even neighborhood to take out a ninja, fire is your answer. Though some modern ninja outfits are made of flame-retardant materials, ninjas are still vulnerable to fire, especially around the eyes and through smoke inhalation. But there are major limitations. Flame throwers are cumbersome, especially indoors. Molotov cocktails pack a punch, but they're awkward. If a ninja spots either weapon in the open, he or she will target the container with a hail of *shuriken*. Still, catching the ninja by surprise with a powerful burst of flame can mean "game over." If you attempt to use a Molotov cocktail indoors, be sure to keep a fire extinguisher close at hand.

EASE OF USE	EFFECTIVENESS	LETHALITY	OVERALL ANTI-NINJA RATING
4	8	8	20/30 (NOT RECOMMENDED)

MODERN DEFENSE

Ninjas are capable of working around most modern defenses such as surveillance systems, robotic weaponry and unmanned drones.

However, you should have a few basic items on hand to give you more of an advantage.

NIGHT VISION DEVICE (NVD)

The statistics are staggering. Over 87 percent of all ninja attacks occur either at night or during the dim hours of twilight. These assassins have mastered the art of using darkness as cover, stealing in and out of crime scenes as mere shadows in a wash of black. You can reduce the efficacy of those tactics by using night vision goggles or a night vision scope. Practice with the NVD. They can distort vision and disorient the novice user.

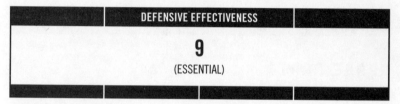

DEFENSIVE EFFECTIVENESS
9
(ESSENTIAL)

BODY ARMOR

As we've discussed earlier in this guide, body armor is of the greatest importance when facing a ninja. Modern armor can stop anything from a knife (or sword) attack to a high-caliber bullet. Your best bet is to purchase a quality vest and then improvise enough armor to cover your vulnerable arms, legs and neck. (Hint: Modern suitcases are often made of ballistic nylon to guard against reckless baggage handlers; if you can deal with cutting up your $400 garment bag, chances are your limbs will thank you later.)

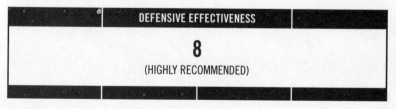

DEFENSIVE EFFECTIVENESS
8
(HIGHLY RECOMMENDED)

FIRST AID & FIELD DRESSINGS

Expecting to survive a ninja attack unscathed is out of the question. You should be prepared to deal with everything from deep bruises to deep gashes. Wear a small first-aid kit on your belt at all times. It should contain antiseptic, bandages and tourniquets. A more extensive first-aid kit should be close at hand as well.

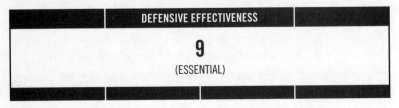

DEFENSIVE EFFECTIVENESS
9
(ESSENTIAL)

SPARE PARTS

If you have the resources to procure spare vital organs that are compatible with your own, keep as many on hand as possible. Designate a separate refrigerator for the storage of the organs, replenishing them whenever they pass their expiration dates. Ninjas will often strike the lungs, kidneys or hard-to-reach pancreas during targeted attacks. Keep the number of a good surgeon in your phonebook and enough immunosuppressive drugs to prevent organ rejection.

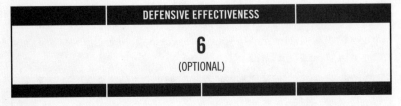

DEFENSIVE EFFECTIVENESS
6
(OPTIONAL)

CHAPTER 7

BUYING TIME: NEGOTIATING WITH AND BEFRIENDING YOUR NINJA ASSASSIN

Ninjas are complex people. But deep inside of every ninja is a ninja child, crying out for their ninja master.

—*Hisoka Shimizu-Brown, criminal psychologist*

✳ ✳ ✳

There is a chance you can successfully escape a ninja attack without any blood being shed. Ninjas, despite their incredibly disciplined self-control, nearly perfect bodies, impeccable tea-brewing techniques, and capacity for murder, are still sensitive human beings to some regard. Their emotional core tends to be buried beneath years of rigorous mental training and brutal conditioning. But their all-too-human emotions still exist.

Every ninja has at least one weakness. If you're able to identify the door to your assailant's inner self, you may be able to manipulate the situation and increase the chances of your own survival.

Take note, however: Negotiating with your ninja assassin should be used as a LAST RESORT OPTION. In the last 850 years, only 15 people have successfully talked ninjas out of completing their mission. But when it comes to a life-or-death situation, one final plea, seductive suggestion, or an irresistibly attractive counteroffer just may save your life.

The following section is a small sampling of ninja weaknesses gathered over the past century. What does the ninja find irresistible? What stimuli will unravel the ninja's rigid sense of discipline? What makes the ninja tick? What makes the ninja cry? And finally, what makes the ninja happy? Choose your manipulation tactic based on your own personal attributes and skills, the location of the attack, and the personal qualities you can deduce from your assailant.

NINJA WEAKNESSES

Ninjas have spent a lifetime training to subdue, control and ultimately free themselves of the Five Weaknesses. Therefore, targeting a ninja's sense of fear, anger, lust, sympathy or greed is extremely difficult and will almost never work. To negotiate with your ninja, you must be crafty, subtle, original or just straight-up filthy rich.

Fear: Ninjas are faster, stronger, smarter and better than you. Do not attempt to frighten a ninja; it will merely provoke laughter.

Anger: Ninjas can willfully distribute the chemical components of anger throughout their bodies, morphing themselves into an even deadlier and unstoppable force. As their heartbeats elevate and their blood engorges their muscles to capacity, their adrenal glands secrete incredible doses of adrenaline throughout their body, turning your ninja assailant into a chemically charged killing machine. Provoking anger in ninjas will cause them to grow in size, strength and agility.

Sympathy: During a ninja attack, most targets are reduced to blubbering babies, begging their attacker for compassion and forgiveness. Ninjas do not have empathy for non-ninjas. Turning on the water works will only serve as ninja-sword lubrication.

NINJA TRAINING: "SLAUGHTER THE PIG"

During early childhood, every ninja goes through a special training technique called "Slaughter the Pig." Young ninjas-in-training are instructed to kill their pet pig and prepare it for dinner. Having befriended the adorable swine, the ninjas inevitably resist. Over the next few weeks, their parents insist, refusing to eat any food until their child has slaughtered their pet pig. The child must choose between starving his or her own parents and murdering the beloved pet pig. Though a heartbreaking decision, the child always choose to slaughter his or her beloved friend. Because of this training technique, using pathos to deal with a ninja will have adverse effects. After all, the last time they felt empathy, they almost killed their parents.

Lust: Ninja lust is one weakness that *can* be targeted. Because lust is the most primitive of the Five Weaknesses, it is more inflexibly ingrained in the human psyche and is therefore hardest for the ninja to eliminate. If you're especially sexy and alluring, any warm-blooded ninja may be unable to resist a well-designed seduction. The following is a list of common ninja turn-ons:

- Cloudy, moonless nights
- Being dominated
- A bottle of hot *sake*
- Naked sushi
- Blindfolds
- Leather masks
- Flirtatious sword fights
- Certain yoga-based Kama Sutra positions, such as Upward-Facing Dog, Snuggly Snake or Opportunistic Hippopotamus.

A well-executed seduction will usually involve a number of the above items. Be creative and confident when approaching your ninja assassin.

Greed: At least one part of the ninja is motivated by greed. This is, after all, a *hired* killer who commits the immoral act of murder for cold cash. If you have the means, you *may* be able to end the attack by offering a particularly irresistible counteroffer. However, the success of a *ryu* is determined by its ability to consistently carry out all of its jobs and maintain good ratings on Yelp. A ninja working for a larger *ryu* may be unwilling to risk possible demotion, alienation, excommunication or even execution for a few extra bucks. Bribes should be supplied in Japanese yen.

NINJA CRAVINGS

Strangely, despite being among the most disciplined people on the planet, most ninjas have a few cravings that they have great difficulty resisting. Some are predictable, others just downright strange.

Quality Herbal Green Tea: The ninja is the consummate fine tea connoisseur. A well-brewed green tea made from high-quality imported leaves is virtually irresistible for almost all ninjas. As ninjas rely so heavily on their olfactory sense during battle, no strongly scented tea will remain unnoticed by a ninja assailant.

Ninjas are at their most vulnerable while under the meditative trance of a green tea binge. Once ninjas take their first sip, they won't stop until they've finished the entire pot. Thus, always keep a kettle brewing and have the finest fresh tea leaves stored in a cool, dry place.

Oreos: For reasons not entirely understood, all ninjas are Oreo cookie addicts. They especially like the cream-filled center. When your assailant initiates his or her attack, fight sword with snack.

Twister: Have you ever seen a group of ninjas playing Twister? It's the most beautiful thing in the world. Since the advent of the annual Twister Tournament Brussels, a ninja has taken away

the gold medal 27 out of 28 times. Twister is used as recreational training in almost all ninja *ryu*, though play is usually banned for ninjas older than 15. If a ninja sees a Twister board during an attack, he or she will be overwhelmed with Proustian nostalgia and an insatiable desire to play the game. Twister is especially effective if you're being attacked by more than one ninja. The game can easily tie up four ninjas for quite a while.

NINJA ANNOYANCES

There are very few things that aggravate a composed ninja. As of the printing of this manual, this is the only one that has been confirmed:

Bad Ninja Movies: For obvious reasons, ninjas cannot stand movies that inaccurately portray their kind. Using an old VCR or projector, play a looped flick such as *Beverley Hills Ninja*, *Full Metal Ninja* or *Three Ninjas Kick Back*. Ninjas will suspend battle until they've figured out how to turn off the movie.

YOUR ASSAILANT, YOUR FRIEND: TOUCHING ON NOSTALGIA

Most ninjas are pushed from a young age and pressured to grow up faster than is usual, and as a result their childhoods are unnaturally brief. Imagine the nostalgia you feel for your own childhood: As an adult, work is tough, life is filled with stress. Sometimes you want to curl up into a fetal ball and be hugged by your mom. You wish you could go back to the way things were when you were a child.

Now imagine life as a ninja. Instead of working as a lawyer, bartender, construction worker or a truck driver, you're a hired assassin. You deal with death on a daily basis. The tiniest mistake could cost you your life, or leave you severely injured. The pressure is unbelievable, almost unbearably so. The only joy in your life was the few years before you learned to kill. Your childhood was brief, but stands in such stark contrast to the remainder of your life that it stands out in your memory.

Attempt to play up to a ninja's sense of nostalgia, stocking play swords or wooden ninja stars in plain sight. The ninja will immediately be transported back to a bygone time in life. This is a good time to initiate your negotiation using a soft, soothing voice.

BEFRIENDING WITH FOOD

The ninja's initial impression of you is the most important. Throughout the attack you must treat your assailant with kindness and reverence, and be especially courteous even as you face death. Assure him or her that you understand and appreciate what he or she has come to do, and promise that you'll die with grace and honor; the ninja, in turn, will admire your composure and fearlessness.

Once you've earned the respect of your assailant, quickly persuade him or her to join you for a final dinner. Offer enough *sake* to take the edge off the situation.

Once the ninja has warmed up to you, make a few jokes. Laugh at any jokes the ninja makes, even if they're not particularly funny or in English. As you're speaking, try gently touching the ninja's arm while looking him or her directly in the eye.

If your conversation falters, throw in a comment about how atrocious you find poorly brewed teas. If the dinner is unsuccessful, the ninja will thank you for a "pleasant meal" and kill you.

If, however, your dinner is successful, chances are you've successfully befriended a ninja. Not an easy feat! In addition to being killed, you now have a thoroughly trained ninja as your friend! Just imagine the things you can do with a highly lethal ninja *tomodachi*.

HELPFUL JAPANESE

Hello	*Konnichiwa*
Please	*Kudasai*
Good evening, ninja	*Kombanwa, shinobi-no-mono*
Nice to meet you, handsome	*Hajimemashite, hansamuna*
Dinner	*Bangohan*

CHAPTER 8

NINJA MYTH
AND REALITY

Project STEALTH has collected an enormous amount of data about ninjas, spanning back over 300 years. The most important part they can play is to educate the public about the ninja threat, dispelling rumors and delivering facts.

✳ ✳ ✳

THIRTEEN FASCINATING FACTS ABOUT NINJAS

- Ninjas do not move during mating. They're stimulated to orgasm by the mind alone. Most Eastern countries identify "wet or erotic dreams" to be, in actuality, ninja rape.

- An American household will unknowingly host an average of 2.5 ninja "threats" per year.

- On April 13, 1865, Abraham Lincoln accidentally uncovered a ninja training school in his tool shed. The next evening he went to the theater.

continued on next page

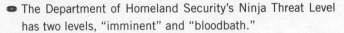

continued from previous page

- The Department of Homeland Security's Ninja Threat Level has two levels, "imminent" and "bloodbath."

- World census shows that the life expectancy of a ninja is approximately 118 years old, making them, on average, the longest-living warriors by 56 years.

- "Waldo" of the popular Where's Waldo? series was originally a failed ninja who ended up relocating around the world to escape his vengeful *ryu*.

- Female ninjas are capable of bearing children until death.

- In January 1992, George H. W. Bush threw up on the Prime Minister of Japan after eating "bad sushi."

- Ninjas learn to assassinate before they learn to walk.

- During urination, ninjas place their entire torso beneath the waterline of the toilet to avoid making any sound.

- The notorious "Spanish Flu" of 1914 that killed over 50 million people worldwide was originally thought to be a ninja-turned-serial-killer named Toyotomi Hayasho. At the time, he was thought to be the scariest thing ever conceived.

- To save on weight, ninjas forgo having kidneys.

- The barbaric torture technique of waterboarding was originally taken from the more advanced ninja *manako-etchi*, where a ninja would stare at the detainee until asphyxiation set in.

CAN NINJAS FLY?

For millennia a debate has raged over whether or not ninjas possess the ability to fly. Today, popular movies depicting kung fu battles in tree tops and lofty sword fights on roofs have fueled speculation into a wildfire of rumor. For those few who have seen ninjas in action and survived to tell about it, these rumors are hard to deny.

"Not flying exactly, he looked as though he was swimming, just swimming through the air; it was effortless . . . gravity just a minor inconvenience. His feet would tap the ground every few yards, only to spring off again," says Phil Hemmings, an Annapolis construction worker who witnessed a ninja escape through a busy construction site in 1997.

In reality, ninja movements are more closely a refined version of the urban phenom "parkour" or "free running." The ninja will move with apparent effortlessness through an urban landscape, employing stationary objects to launch efficient acrobatic movements that can help them avoid cumbersome obstacles such as cars, Mack trucks or buildings.

NINJAS CAN'T CATCH YOU WHEN YOU'RE ON FIRE

Recently, this rumor has spread on the internet like a wildfire intentionally set by ninjas. It's absurd and entirely untrue. Unfortunately, countless people have tried to escape an imminent ninja attack through foolhardy self-immolation. Before you grab for the gas can yourself, keep a few things in mind:

- Ninjas do not easily burn and know no fear of fire.
- Ninja swords are forged in fires hotter than the furnaces of hell. They're fireproof. Ninjas will still stab you.
- Being on fire makes escaping unseen and unscathed much more difficult.
- Your family can still collect life insurance after a ninja attack. Ninja induced–suicides are generally not covered.

NINJAS VS. PIRATES

It seems a bit absurd, but ninjas are often compared to or pitted against pirates in popular culture. The only time that pirates have ever had the misfortune of coming across a clan of ninjas was in September 1792, when a band of heavily armed Spanish buccaneers accidentally boarded a vessel transporting a squad of ninjas en route to a mission in Haiti.

Twelve pirates boarded the schooner containing just four ninjas. Not a shot was fired before all 12 of the marauders ended up in the drink. The survivors, despite being just a few hundred yards from the shoreline, chose to drown in the Caribbean waters rather than live with the horror of what they had just seen. When it comes to ninjas vs. pirates, the victor is clear.

NINJAS THROUGHOUT HISTORY

The following anecdotes outline the subtle yet profound effect ninjas have had on world history.

SHAKESPEARE'S "LOST YEARS" AND HIS "SOJOURN TO JAPAN"

On February 2, 1585, William Shakespeare's wife, Anne Hathaway, gave birth to twins, after which the bard mysteriously disappeared until springing up on the theater scene in 1592. Historians have bickered over Shakespeare's activity during these "Lost Years" for centuries, but recently the "Sojourn to Japan" theory garnered much attention.

Although there has been no direct mention of his name in any Japanese documentation during that time, there is extensive mention of a やりのシェーカー , which can be roughly translated as Mr. Spear Shaker, a witty, well-read Englishman who lived as an English tutor in the central mountains of Japan. The evidence runs deeper than that as well. No fewer than 17 of Shakespeare's 38 surviving plays contain "significant similarities in part or in whole" to several traditional Japanese ninja and samurai tales. Furthermore, of these 17, 6 are considered by some scholars to be "direct retellings of ninja mythologies and legends."

The following are just two examples of Shakespeare's works drawn directly from the ninja canon.

Romeo and Juliet: Possibly the most well-known of all Shakespeare's plays, the plot of *Romeo and Juliet* parallels the famous ninja story *Rokuro and Jun: A Ninja Tragedy*. The story, imparted to all young ninjas as they enter puberty, is a parable advising against passion, lust and love.

Rokuro is the sixth son in a powerful ninja family; Jun is the obedient daughter of a rival *ryu*. One evening, the two teenagers meet in the woods and immediately fall in love. Their love blossoms with meteoric intensity and they plan to marry and leave Japan. However, the night of their wedding, they both receive missions from their respective clans. The intended victims—each other. Unable to kill one another and incapable of disobeying a *jonin*'s direct order, the teens draw their blades and commit *seppuku* independently.

Shakespeare removed the ninja aspect from his adaptation, fearing the West would not find the "suicides for honor" believable and because he had a penchant for additional teen angst. Shakespeare also went so far as to borrow lines from the original version, such as, "For never was a story of such deadly *hambo*, than this of Jun and her Rokuro."

Of course, in the end of *Rokuro and Jun,* the families do not make amends, but rather descend into two centuries of brutal warfare.

Hamlet: The story of Hamlet, one of the planet's most famous, was clearly borrowed from the ninja parable *Hamarito*.

The tale begins when young Hamarito awakes in a cold sweat, having "sensed" that his father, the *ryu's jonin*, has been murdered by Hamarito's uncle Katsumo. The next day Katsumo assumes power and marries Hamarito's mourning mother.

In a rage, Hamarito plans to kill Katsumo. Katsumo learns of Hamarito's plot and arranges to have him killed instead. The night before the fight, Hamarito contemplates suicide, quoted as saying, "Live by the sword, or die by the blade?" which Shakespeare turned into the slightly less poetic "to be or not to be. . . ." The fight that ensues lives on in ninja infamy like none other. Unlike the final scenes in *Hamlet*, no poison blades or swords are used. Instead, both men unleash the most magnificent barrage of *shuriken* (ninja stars) in human history, killing each other and the 300 spectators who come to watch.

This ninja tale was told in clans as a parable advising against jealousy and standing too close to violent entertainment.

Many historians dispute the verity of Shakespeare's "Sojourn to Japan," pointing to the Jungian theory that all mythologies, basic characters, and plots are so intrinsically rooted in the human psyche that analogous parables often arise in isolated cultures. While this argument makes superficial sense, anything more than a cursory comparison of Shakespeare's works proves that the bard was, like so many other famous writers and playwrights, heavily influenced by the ninja.

THE NINJA CUPID

As a young ninja, Hiroshi Kurasawa showed almost preternatural abilities in the art of alchemy; using crude ingredients, he invented complex deadly poisons and powerful medicinal concoctions. Because of his unique skill, he was considered one of Makagami *ryu's* most respected warriors. His poisons had killed thousands of enemies, while his medicines had saved tens of lives. While researching a new poison, however, a horrendous explosion left his face terribly disfigured.

When Hiroshi came of age, he fell in love with one of his village's most beautiful girls, Kameko, but when he finally approached her, she cringed in horror. He realized then that he was a hideous monster; what girl would want to marry him?

Heartbroken, Hiroshi retreated to his laboratory with the intention of creating a love potion. After three years of experimentation and research, Hiroshi discovered a number of ingredients: horny goat weed, python heart, oysters, alcohol, ginkgo biloba, and saffron. But the concoction was unfinished. It was while on a medicinal voyage to China that Hiroshi discovered the perfect base for his potion: tiger penis. He returned home with 50 tiger penises and manufactured a lifetime's supply of history's most powerful aphrodisiac.

That night Hiroshi hid in Kameko's yard. When she returned home, he shot her in the buttocks with an arrow he had dipped into the potion. He jumped from his perch and ran to her aid. The strong aphrodisiac quickly entered her bloodstream, and by the time he reached her she was overcome with lust. They made love and were married one month later. Hiroshi, for the rest of his life, fought anger with love, shooting warriors with his love potion, and turning murder missions into libidinous love fests.

THE SAKE BOMB

The *sake* bomb. Cold beer, hot *sake*. Delicious. Exhilarating. A rite of passage for sushi-grubbing 21-year-olds around the world. And a drink with an origin as dark as moonless midnight atop Mount Fuji.

On a cold night in December 1882, the shady German emissary Burkhard Brechstein was enjoying a cold glass of Bohemian lager with a small group of friends at his home near Sapporo. Unbeknownst to him, a ninja assassin had infiltrated his intimate gathering and had brewed up a batch of venomous *sake* to serve to the notorious statesman.

Unfortunately for the assassin, when he handed the poisoned rice wine to his intended victim, the inebriated foreigner clumsily dropped his *sake* cup into his pint glass. Laughing heartily, he gulped down the alcoholic concoction with no ill effect. Why? Centuries later it was speculated that the acidity of the beer's hops neutralized the crude poison, allowing the German to drink freely.

Astonished, the ninja returned to his *ryu* with stories of a "magic" libation that could protect against the strongest ninja neurotoxins.

Four years later, that ninja, Seibei Nakagawa, opened his first brewery in the same town in which he had failed to kill Brechstein. From that day forward, the *sake* bomb would come to symbolize a "long life and protection from all ills, with the exception of headaches, poor sexual choices and projectile vomiting." Every year, the Yebisu *ryu* celebrates the accidental invention with a series of nine *sake* bombs followed by the ritualistic ninja-starring of passersby.

YOSHIMI YOYO

The yo-yo—toy, household annoyance, complex tool of death— was invented by a 13-year-old female ninja. In 1527, eight-year-old Yoshimi Yoyo watched from a treetop as her parents were brutally slaughtered by a band of samurai sent by a ruthless shogun named Takami. After murdering everybody she loved, the samurai warriors set fire to the village and rode off into the moonlight. Yoshimi, a brash and impetuous child, followed them in secret all the way to Kyoto.

The next morning she prostrated herself in front of Shogun Takami's palace. When asked, she informed the servants that her parents were dead and she had no place to live. Taking pity on the poor, young girl, the staff invited her into the palace and hid her from the powerful lord.

For years she worked the palace grounds and buried her desire for vengeance against Takami. She, after all, was not allowed to touch any weapons and her target. How would she overpower Lord Takami and his bodyguards?

Four years later, while toiling in the sewing room, Yoshimi invented a yo-yo by looping thread around an iron cloth weight. She became proficient at difficult tricks like "walking the dog," "skinning the cat," "splitting the bamboo" and "assassinating the lay person." Assuming it was a game, the shogun's bodyguards permitted Yoshimi to practice, even in the presence of the shogun.

One day, she noticed the strolling shogun flanked by only one guard instead of his normal 15. Springing into action, she flung her yo-yo at the sword of the younger guard, ensnaring the sheathed blade and drawing it quickly to her. In one fluid flick of the wrist, she cleanly beheaded the man who had taken her family. She turned to the astonished guard and flung her yo-yo at the disarmed samurai. It coiled around his neck like a snake and, within half a minute, the man was dead.

To this date, the legend of Yoshimi Yoyo still lives on in the hearts of the many children who play with the devious, spinning toys.

CHAPTER 9

CONCLUSION

If anything, from reading this book you've gained a healthy sense of extreme paranoia. The facts are as cold as the blade of a ninja sword. Ninjas are everywhere. Eventually you'll be targeted. Your time to prepare is limited. There is not much you can do; the ninja has already outsmarted you. Which brings us back to the ancient Japanese proverb at the beginning of this book:

If you come to a fork in a road, grab a knife.

> —*Proverb found at the Oyaji Ninjutsu School*
> *Hachimantai, Japan, c. 15th century A.D.*

✳ ✳ ✳

The saying is ominous, to say the least. It implies danger ahead, no matter which road you take. But the true surprise is in the easily understood pun. Though silverware, specifically the fork, has been around in some form or another since ancient Greece, the first sets arrived in Asia more than 200 years after this proverb was crafted. Did the ninja know the fork was coming—in more ways than one?

OTHER ULYSSES PRESS BOOKS

Blonde Walks into a Bar: The 4,000 Most Hilarious, Gut-Busting Gags, One-Liners and Jokes

Jonathan Swan, $14.95

Unapologetically funny and irreverent, *Blonde Walks into a Bar* holds nothing back as it delivers laugh after laugh.

Caution: Funny Signs Ahead

Compiled by RoadTrip America, $11.95

Anyone who has ever hit the open road has seen a sign that sends them into hysterics. *Caution: Funny Signs Ahead* is the ultimate collection of these accidentally entertaining bits of roadside Americana.

Dirty Japanese: Everyday Slang from "What's Up?" to "F*%# Off!"

Matt Fargo, $10.00

Even in traditionally minded Japan, slang from its edgy pop culture constantly enters into common usage. This book fills in the gap between how people really talk in Japan and what Japanese language students are taught.

The Ginormous Book of Dirty Jokes: Over 1,000 Sick, Filthy and X-Rated Jokes

Rudy A. Swale, $12.95

There are some jokes that can never be repeated in front of one's mother. That doesn't mean the jokes aren't funny. Generally it means they're laugh-out-loud hilarious! *The Ginormous Book of Dirty Jokes* offers the biggest, baddest, badassest collection of these off-color quips.

Man Walks into a Bar: Over 6,000 of the Most Hilarious Jokes, Funniest Insults and Gut-Busting One-Liners

Stephen Arnott & Mike Haskins, $14.95

Man Walks into a Bar is packed full of quick and easy jokes that are as simple to remember and repeat as they are funny.

Seriously Sick Jokes: The Most Disgusting, Filthy, Offensive Jokes from the Vile, Obscene, Disturbed Minds of b3ta.com

Rob Manuel, $10.95

Seriously Sick Jokes is a lewd, crude and absolutely filthy collection that will have readers cringing between bouts of uncontrollable laughter.

The Ultimate Dirty Joke Book

Mike Oxbent & Harry P. Ness, $11.95

The Ultimate Dirty Joke Book holds back nothing and guarantees outrageous laughs.

To order these books call 800-377-2542 or 510-601-8301, fax 510-601-8307, e-mail ulysses@ulyssespress.com, or write to Ulysses Press, P.O. Box 3440, Berkeley, CA 94703. All retail orders are shipped free of charge. California residents must include sales tax. Allow two to three weeks for delivery.

ABOUT THE AUTHORS

Sam Kaplan (born Samurai Kaplan) is an author, casual exerciser, grilled-cheese aficionado and hard-core ninja expert. An avid fan of Teenage Mutant Ninja Turtles since the age of six, he has never been successfully attacked by a ninja. He lives in Oakland with his pet water buffalo, George.

Phoebe Bronstein was born and raised in Oakland, California—a hotbed for ninja activity—and has recently returned to the Bay Area after getting a master's degree in *ninjutsu* literature. She has spent time traveling and living in Central America and England, where she studied the brutal effects of ninja violence in both English and Spanish.

Keith Riegert is a senior intern at Project STEALTH's Northern California Department of Counter-Ninja Security. Through his significant catering duties, he has overheard enough to consider himself an amateur expert on ninjas. He currently lives in a secure apartment in Oakland, California.